UNLEASH

YOUR CRAZY SEXY BRAIN

UMAR HAMEED

ULEASH

YOUR CRAZY SEXY BRAIN

Printed in the U.S.A.

First printing 2016

Foreword

Hack Your Mind for Peak Performance

The single most important element that will determine your success in sales, leadership and in life is your mindset.

Your mindset is a set of attitudes and beliefs that influence and shape your behaviors. According to scientific research, we start to create these attitudes and beliefs the moment we're born. You store them in a particular area of your brain, called the prefrontal cortex. This is where neural connections form into cognitive elements, memories, and associated feelings from past experiences. Some call this the executive function of the brain -- I like to think of the prefrontal cortex as our "inner CEO."

Over the past 30 years I studied high performing executives, athletes, entertainers, business leaders and discussed what I've found with psychologists, psychiatrists and high performance coaches. Over time I uncovered the specific beliefs and behaviors that create a peak performance mindset. High achievers consciously create a belief system that helps them cope effectively with difficult situations at work. They're also able to identify and eliminate the performance blockers that might stand in the way of their success.

We can see these traits in great leaders. Take Bill McDermott, a former Xerox account rep who is now the CEO of SAP, a company with a $105 billion market cap. When he worked at Xerox, he took over Puerto Rico – the worst performing territory in the country – and moved it to first place within 12 months simply by changing the team's mindset.

Your mindset is also the key to unlock your physical performance. For example, Dr. Becca Levy at Yale University found that when people create a positive mindset about ageing, they would actually live 7.6 years longer than people with a mindset that's negative. So, if you hold the belief in your prefrontal cortex that age is a matter of progressive deterioration, chances are that your body will shut down 7.6 years earlier.

Another example of a person with a peak performance mindset is Dan Waldschmidt, author of the book Edgy Conversations. He recently ran a 100-mile race (nearly the equivalent of nearly four consecutive marathons) and finished first, beating more than 150 people (only 10% of the runners actually finished the race). Dan uses two high-performance coaches that help him with his mind-body connection to get his body to achieve progressively greater results.

When Dan wakes up in the morning, he begins the day with a positive affirmation: "Today I will do whatever it takes, for as long as it takes, to achieve my goals." Dan also meditates every day to clear his mind and connect with his true self. When the going gets tough, he Dan says to himself, "Every day in every way I am getter better and better by the choices I make and the actions I take."

Peak Performers like Dan Waldschmidt or Bill McDermott remind us that we can direct our minds to become a powerful, positive, and productive force. To hack your mindset and boost sales think about taking charge of the executive function of your brain.

In this book, Umar Hameed shares many tools to reprogram your mindset so you can transform your limiting behaviors into empowering one's. Unleash Your Crazy Sexy Brain gives you the strategies you need to make massive improvements in every area of your life.

Gerhard Gschwandtner

Publisher Selling Power Magazine

Contents

Forword: By Gerhard Gschwandtner i

Introduction 3

Chapter One: The Anatomy Of Change 8

Chapter Two: How Your Brain Works 12

Chapter Three: A Metaphor For Success 18

Chapter Four: The Sales Process 23

Chapter Five: The Power Of Beliefs 29

Chapter Six: The Model Of The World............................... 34

Chapter Seven: Beliefs In Business Teams 39

Chapter Eight: Limiting Beliefs 44

Chapter Nine: Hot-Wired Processes................................. 48

Chapter Ten: Inner Conflicts.. 54

Chapter Eleven: Communication Mastery 58

Chapter Twelve: Anchoring Excellence............................. 67

Chapter Thirteen: Getting Unstuck 73

Chapter Fourteen: Psycho-Geography 79

Chapter Fifteen: The Disney Technique............................. 86

Chapter Sixteen: The Einstein Principle............................. 96

Chapter Seventeen: The Tesla Effect 103

Chapter Eighteen: Building A Stronger Team 109

Conclusion.. 138

Free Advanced Mind Training 142

About The Author 143

Introduction

This was the defining moment that changed the direction of my life. Six months earlier I had taken up squash. I loved everything about the game. The stamina, the speed and the skill made it a highly addictive activity. Each time I played a game I worked hard. I had passion and I loved every second of it. The only problem was that I sucked at it. I mean I was dreadful.

A couple of months later I got a good bit better. In another month or two I got better still. One day it occurred to me that I was making massive improvements in squash while I was coasting in my computer consulting business.

It was odd because I loved my work and I worked hard to improve my performance. But no matter how hard I tried I seemed to deliver average results.

One day I was complaining to John, my friend and mentor, that I loved squash and my business. I work hard at both but I was only improving my performance in squash. Why was I stuck in my business? John suggested that I go see Una Elliott, a Neuro-Linguistic Programming (NLP) practitioner.

I told Una about my dilemma; squash good, business bad. In an hour and 30 minutes she helped me get a breakthrough that changed my life from that day on. I knew in my heart of hearts that something profound had changed within me. Whatever mental block was making me coasted in my business career was gone. As I walked out of that session, I made a promise to myself that I would learn how to change human behavior.

The very next day I started making better decisions in my business. My level of intensity at work went way up. I felt a state of flow that made growing my business easier. I truly felt that there was no stopping me. I could achieve any goal that I set my mind to.

Within a year I decided to move from Toronto Canada to Silicon Valley the Mecca of computing. Over the years I worked myself up from being an entry level account executive to starting my own sales and marketing consulting firm.

It turns out that Silicon Valley, is also the birthplace of NLP. During my time in the Valley, I got certified as a practitioner of NLP and then as a master practitioner of NLP. This new skill set allowed me to excel in all areas of my life especially, in my ability to sell.

The Human Paradox

Most salespeople are continually looking to improve their performance. They read books, go to seminars and look for motivational material that will drive them to do better. Sales managers are continually looking for ways to improve salesperson performance. Sales managers will offer vacations and cash rewards for improved performance. They will also use negative motivation like "you will be fired!" to drive better sales performance from their sales reps.

Both salespeople and their managers want them to better. The problem is very few salespeople actually improve their performance in any significant manner. I wanted to solve this paradox. The question that I was desperately trying to answer was what really stops salespeople from improving their performance.

To get insights into this situation, I interviewed the best salespeople I could find. After just a dozen interviews I found a pattern. Great salespeople possess three areas of mastery. One, they have the sales skills to do the job really well. Two, they think strategically which allows them to work smarter and outperform their competitors. Three, they have the right mindset that allows them to use their sales skills more effectively. All this enables them to wholeheartedly take the actions they need to fearlessly follow their strategic vision.

The combination of skill set, strategy and mindset drive them to achieve exceptional results. In our business landscape, there are a ton of great sales training companies to teach salespeople how to sell (sales skills). There are business consultants that teach salespeople and organizations how to think strategically so they become more effective. But, there are very few places to learn how transform a salesperson's mindset. This book is designed to teach salespeople how to develop a stronger sales mindset.

I have been invited to 12 countries to speak at business conferences to talk about the human element.

Business leaders are hungry to learn what drives a salesperson's behavior and how to change it so they become exceptional.

Over the past 12 years I have helped thousands of salespeople break through their barriers so they sell more effectively. I wrote this book to share my finding with you so you can break through your barriers and become a better salesperson.

Chapter One

THE ANATOMY OF CHANGE

More than 30 years ago – when she was just 9 years old – Sonia experienced one of the most significant days of her life. Her mother was going out on her first date since being divorced six months earlier. "Just keep the doors and windows locked and you'll be fine," her mother said.

Sonia wanted to be brave, but she became increasingly anxious after her mother left. She had never been left alone before. A short time later, she heard someone walking up the front steps toward the front door. She raced to the kitchen where she pulled out a large knife from the butcher-block cutlery set on the counter. Knife in hand, she ran to the bathroom and slammed the door shut. She waited in the dark.

I met Sonia recently. She is the CEO of a successful company and she's especially proud of her management team. It took Sonia two years to find the right people – people who had the drive, passion and expertise – to help her build the company.

Yet, here's the problem: Sonia is a world-class micromanager. She must involve herself with every decision her team makes. Her actions have alienated members of her team and slowed the overall operation of the company. Sonia, at least, recognized this problem. She participated in a workshop that focused on delegation skills, and she even hired a personal coach. Still, nothing changed.

When Sonia came to see me, she spoke about her compulsion to micromanage.

I asked her to think of an instance when she felt the need to satisfy this compulsion. "Just the other day," she said, "I was talking with a client and something was going wrong. And, I felt the urge to take charge."

"Sonia, in your mind, go back to that event and visualize what you saw," I said. "Listen to what you heard – your client's voice, any sounds that were present, and your inner thoughts. When you do that, you begin to feel what you were feeling then.

"Oh my God," Sonia said. "I'm feeling it now. There's a weird feeling in my belly."

By utilizing a tool I learned from neuroscience, I helped Sonia to link that feeling in her mid-section with her unconscious mind. I said to her unconscious mind: "This is a distinctive feeling that you are experiencing – when have you felt it before?"

If I had addressed Sonia's conscious mind, the response would have been: "I don't know." The unconscious mind, however, records everything. As soon as I asked her about the feeling, her mind took her back to that event 30 years before.

That night, as she hid in the bathroom holding the large kitchen knife, Sonia had a thought: "To my mother, men are more important than me." With that thought, she created a powerful belief: "The only person in the entire world whom I can truly trust is me." It was that belief that drove her behavior for three decades.

Using that NLP tool, I showed Sonia how to change that belief. After a 90-minute session, it became visibly apparent that something profound had happened to Sonia. As she left the session, I asked her to take notice of anything that felt different.

Sonia called me a few days later and said: "I'm not sure what you did, but it's like 100 pounds have been lifted off my shoulders." She also said her urge to micromanage was gone, and for the first time in her life, she was truly enjoying her accomplishments.

Change happens in an instant. In our culture, we think that change is difficult, takes a long time, and may never occur despite our best efforts. The latest advances in neuroscience, however, prove that change can happen quickly and that change is permanent.

Chapter Two

HOW YOUR BRAIN WORKS

At the core of who you are is where you hold your beliefs. You have anywhere from 50,000 to 100,000 beliefs that define you. We have beliefs about everything in our awareness, from cars to coffee to marriage. The problem is that we form the vast number of our beliefs by the age of 7. After that, we develop only an additional 5 percent of our beliefs.

We get our beliefs from parents, uncles and aunts, and teachers. If someone in authority says something believable during our first seven years, that thought goes into our unconscious and becomes a belief that influences our life from then on.

Getting a new belief is as simple as this: One Saturday morning a family goes out car shopping. They arrive at a dealership and Mom says to Dad: "Remember, don't let the salesperson know you like a certain car, otherwise he'll force you to buy it."

Five-year-old Sally, sitting in the backseat, hears this and forms a belief: "Don't trust salespeople."

From that point on, Sally looks for evidence to support this belief. Beliefs become self-fulfilling prophecies. Every time she hears about a salesperson taking advantage of someone, it strengthens her belief. And, if she hears of a salesperson going above and beyond the call of duty, she'll either disregard it or assume the salesperson is only doing it for a nefarious purpose. To consider this information differently would invalidate her belief.

Your brain is an energy hog

Your brain accounts for 2 percent of your body's mass, yet it taps 25 percent of your body's energy. This sounds like a substantial amount of energy. However, it turns out that your brain is lazy. OK, not exactly lazy. Your brain realizes that there are times when you need energy to save your life. You never know when zombies will attack. To conserve energy, your brain uses your beliefs to create a model of the world.

This model is your brain's shorthand for reducing the need to think in general day-to-day activities. As a result, your brain can respond quickly and save energy. Without a model of the world to rely on, you'd have to use 70 percent or more of your available energy.

A good example is driving to work every day: If you had to think carefully about everything you were doing to operate your vehicle and where to turn and how to avoid accidents, you'd be exhausted by the time you arrived. But you don't. Your shorthand model, or autopilot, is operating so you can think about 100 other things and still get to work safely.

The autopilot model dictates most of your behaviors – what you will do and what you won't do. In turn, your behaviors determine the results you achieve. But what happens when the shorthand model causes you to not do the very thing or take the very action that you need to take? Sometimes your autopilot sabotages your success.

The sales mindset

In the world of sales, this is easy to see. Salespeople have dollar amounts attached to their names. For instance, John has a $3 million sales quota. When John is not performing well – as reflected by a low level of sales – his sales manager, Lucy, makes it clear that he must change his behavior, and pretty quickly.

The traditional way to change a salesperson's behavior is to tell John to do things differently, make more cold calls, for instance.

Telling a salesperson to simply change their behavior almost never works. American businesses spend more than $100 billion each year to try to change the behavior of their employees. Yet, these change programs fail more than 70 percent of the time according to a study published by the University of Pennsylvania's Wharton School.

Here's an example: Jack Young, a successful CEO, took a dream and a beat-up truck and turned it into a $100M transportation powerhouse. After Jack sold his company, he opened up a consulting firm that helps other transportation companies grow. His clients pay him a ton of money to get his advice, but their employees seldom follow it. Their limiting beliefs make them resistant to change. To create real change, we have to change the old beliefs first.

Neuroscience to the rescue

Here is another way to look at it: Think of a belief as a black hole that has a massive gravitational force that locks one's behavior in place. No matter how much someone wants to change a behavior, change cannot happen until you identify and transform the underlying belief.

For example: Consider Jane, a salesperson who wants to charge a premium price for her product. In reality, however, the first time a prospect says, "That's too expensive!" Jane drops her price. She knows this is wrong, yet she is powerless to resist the urge to discount. The reason: Despite knowing how to handle such objections, her limiting-beliefs about money force her to lower her price.

This is the most useful model that I have come across that shows the connection between the beliefs someone holds and the results they achieve.

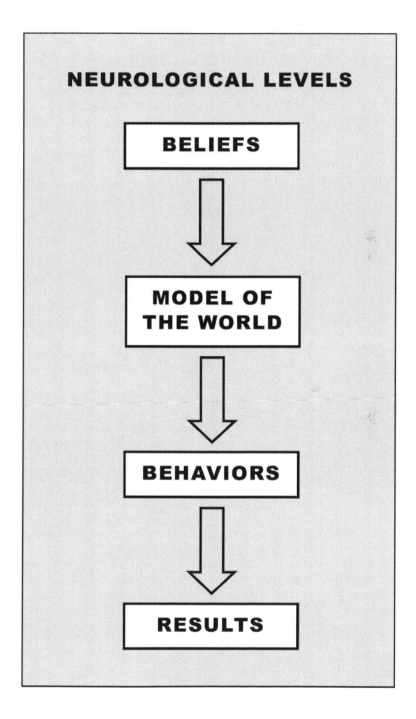

Chapter Three

A METAPHOR FOR SUCCESS

I'm starting this chapter with another story which taught me a powerful way to look at success.Several years ago, I went to a two-day traditional sales-training program. It was a typical training, 95 percent of the material was "same old, same old", with a few nuggets thrown in to make it interesting.

To make the training event memorable, the trainers provided an experiential exercise. Each of us was given a wooden board on which we were asked to describe where we were in our sales careers prior to this training, using pictures, symbols and words.

Next, he asked us use the other side of the board to illustrate what our futures looked like with our new training. We then formed a large circle with the two instructors standing inside it. One instructor held a wooden board. The other instructor showed us how to break it in a single strike. It was both exciting and scary to watch. Each of us would soon have to attempt this feat. Would it hurt?

We all volunteered John, one of our colleagues, to be the first to try breaking the board. We chanted, "John, John, John."

John stepped into the circle and gave his board to the instructor. He pulled back and hit the board, breaking it in one hit. We were ecstatic! Because one of us had actually broken a board, it now seemed possible that we all could.

When willpower doesn't cut it

Jodi was the eighth person to step into the circle. She wanted to be the first woman to break the board. Jodi, for fun, competes in ironman triathlons – events that feature long swims, lengthy bike rides and marathon-distance runs. We all chanted: "Jodi, Jodi, Jodi."

Jodi pulled back and hit the board hard, but it didn't break. However, it was obvious that Jodi had hurt her hand. Not being one to give up, Jodi tried again. On her next attempt, she summoned every ounce of strength and willpower that she had. She pulled back and hit the board even harder than the first time. Again, the board did not break. Feeling humiliation, and pain because she had now severely injured her wrist, she began to cry.

The instructors, not sure what to do, had a choice to make: Stop the exercise and tend to Jodi or push her aside and continue with the group. They chose to continue as a ninth participant entered the circle. Jodi, meanwhile, wandered to a quiet corner of the room.

I left the "circle of death" and went over to her to see if I could help. I told her about my area of expertise in changing human behavior, and that this event could create a trauma that would cripple her self confidence, stopping her for future success. I suggested I show her a technique from Neuro-Linguistic Programming (NLP) that could immediately help and she agreed. Within five minutes, it was done.

Just by looking at her, you could see that something profound had happened. She didn't look upset. The tightness in her face had gone. And, she was smiling.

Having done my good deed for the day, I rejoined the group. By that time, the 23rd or 24th member of the group was about to try to break their board. Jodi stepped back into the circle. This time there wasn't any chanting. Only silence. Jodi handed the instructor her board, and with a single strike, shattered it. She was the only person that day to break a board using her non-dominant hand.

The trick to breaking a board is to imagine your target as being 4 inches behind the board. When you do that, you can break the board easily and it won't hurt – even an 8-year-old could break it.

However, most people are afraid of hitting the board because they expect it to hurt. They end up pulling back on their punches and hurting their hands without breaking the board. Other people hit the board as hard as they can. This often results in the only thing being broken are bones.

The wooden board exercise is a great metaphor for the pursuit of excellence and success.

There are some things in your life that you do effortlessly. This indicates that you are hitting "4 inches" beyond your goal. You have a clear vision of what you want and you fearlessly go after it. You make it look easy.

In some areas of your life, you tend to struggle. You go to hit your "board," and before you strike it, fear emerges, which makes you pull your punch. You end up hurting yourself. Do this enough and you'll likely stop trying.

In other areas of your life, you give it your all and still fail. No matter how hard you try, you're unsuccessful. And, if by chance, you do succeed, it's likely that you'll say: "I don't believe it" – because you don't.

The trick to attaining your dreams is to notice the times when you don't break your particular "board". Those are opportunities to ask yourself: "Why am I not hitting 4 inches past this target?" The answer that emerges will give you a clue as to what belief is holding you hostage. Knowing what you want and fearlessly going for it leads to success and makes you stronger, better and faster.

Chapter Four

THE SALES PROCESS

Ijust did a Google search for "sales training firms" and got 9 million hits. There are tons of sales training programs available, and each promises a magical formula for success. But at their core, they all follow the five basic steps. If you are a sales professional, you already know them.

Get the appointment. A face-to-face or phone-to-phone meeting with a prospect starts the whole process off.

Make the presentation. Communicate your offering to the prospect.

Handle objections. Turning any "no" into a "yes."

Close the sale. Ask prospect to part with his or her money.

Generate more business. Get the customer to buy more from you, while giving you referrals to new prospects.

Once, while doing a presentation for an auditorium full of sales managers, I suggested that the typical sales process, when distilled down to its essence, looks like the one described above. They agreed, despite the fact that they all worked in different companies and industries.

I asked them where in this sales process did their salespeople most often get stuck. And, by what percentage did this reduce they sales potential?

"Getting the appointment" and "closing the sale" tied for first place. The sales managers estimated that if salespeople had difficulties in one of these areas it could cost them about 50 percent of their sales potential. Think about that for a moment. How much more could you sell, if you could get unstuck in every step of the sales process?

Salespeople who have difficulty in getting appointments – no matter how great they might be at closing – will have disappointing sales results because they don't get enough at-bats.

Salespeople who struggle to close sales – no matter how many opportunities they get – will never realize their true sales potential. If you can't close, you might as well go home.

Here's the bottom line: Salespeople who have difficulty in any part of the sales process will suffer in their sales performances. In working with thousands of salespeople, I found that when a salesperson gets unstuck, their performance increases by at least 30 percent.

Let's look at the steps again, with a deeper look at what we as sales managers want our employees to do.

Get the appointment (even though cold calls are scary)

For many salespeople, cold calling is the worst part of the sales process.

Many sales professionals will tell you that cold calling is not worth the effort. In fact, there are books written and entire companies built around how to avoid having to make cold calls.

Steve Richards, the president of Vorsight, would strongly disagree. His company specializes in getting appointments for salespeople who sell high-ticket items, like the leasing of business jets. His team of phone warriors (mostly 20-year-olds) routinely gets CEOs of large companies to set appointments. Steve's team proves cold calling works. If a salesperson believes cold calling won't work, they will end up making sure they fail.

Reluctance to making cold calls comes from one of two areas of weakness. First, salespeople have fear and anxiety that blocks them from doing well on the phone, a mindset issue. In Chapter 10, I'll show you a highly effective method for getting unstuck by transforming fear and anxiety into feeling confident and unstoppable. The second area of weakness is not having an effective process in place. If it is a process issue, go to Amazon and find a good book on cold calling or appointment setting.

Make the presentation (stage fright notwithstanding)

Many salespeople struggle with delivering effective sales presentations. All the studying, role-playing and practice goes out the window when an unconscious belief rears its ugly head.

A common ineffective behavior is the salesperson's compulsion to explain why his company and products are the best in the world. He spends so much time talking about his company and his solution that he fails to uncover his prospect's needs. The result: no connection with the prospect.

Sometimes salespeople feel uncomfortable doing presentations. This discomfort makes their prospects feel uneasy. That discomfort, without a doubt, is hooked to an unconscious belief the salesperson holds probably caused by an old trauma. The result: the uneasy feeling destroys trust which leads to 'no sale!'

Handle objections (no matter what the prospect says)

Numerous studies show that salespeople give up too early. When prospects voice their initial reasons for not doing business, most salespeople can handle the first objection. Hearing additional objections sends them packing.

The salesperson's mindset determines how well she addresses objections. With the right attitude, she can address the first objections in a way that reduces the chances of more objections emerging. If she handles the first objection in a weak manner, their prospects will "smell blood" and be relentless with a wave of follow-up objections.

That right attitude is only possible when your desired behavior aligns with your underlying belief.

Close the sale (you don't ask, you don't get)

I came across an interesting statistic. As you read this book, if you have $10 in your pocket and no debt, you're better off than 25 percent of all Americans. A salesperson's attitudes and beliefs about money have a huge impact on his or her sales performance.

In many families, finances are a taboo topic and beliefs like "money is the root of all evil" are prevalent. In others, the entire sales profession is abhorrent. Even seemingly innocuous programming like "rich people are jerks" can be translated by the mind of a child into a neurosis around money and selling.

Such negative beliefs have a direct impact on a salesperson's ability to ask for the sale. Salespeople who feel uncomfortable asking for money will not be closers. Studies, in fact, show that many salespeople don't ask for the sale directly. They dance around it because it is uncomfortable for them to talk about money.

Trouble getting referrals

You'd be surprised at the number of salespeople who are uncomfortable about asking for referrals. Many years ago, I was working with Paul, a highly successful salesperson, who had difficulty asking for referrals. His average sales transaction was $200,000 and Paul had no problem asking for the sale.

When he tried to ask for a referral, though, his voice would crack as the will to ask evaporated. Just the thought of asking for a referral made Paul uncomfortable, and this feeling would sabotage his efforts every time.

You know which area of the sales process is the most challenging for you. Imagine, if you could master this aspect of your sales process. How much stress would it reduce? How much more would you sell each year? Would there be bonuses and promotions coming your way?

Chapter Five

THE POWER OF BELIEFS

At the very heart of who we are, live the beliefs that define us as human beings. As we discussed in Chapter One, we acquire most of our 50,000-100,000 beliefs by the age of seven. If anyone in authority during those early, open-minded years – a teacher, a parent, or even the Cookie Monster – says something credible, it gets filed in our unconscious system of beliefs.

It's easy to pick up beliefs when you're young. Imagine a family taking a trip from Baltimore to New York City. At the train station in Baltimore, there are a few hundred people milling around. When the family arrives at the station in Manhattan, tens of thousands of people are moving about in all directions. The mother turns to her young daughter, Sally, who is 5 years old and says: "Honey, if you get lost, find a policeman. He'll help you."

That one statement leads Sally to believe that policemen are trustworthy. From that moment on, Sally would look for evidence to validate that belief. Every time she sees a policeman doing something worthy, her belief is strengthened. Her beliefs become so strong that if she'd see a cop behaving badly, she might not even notice. And if she did notice, she'd treat the incident as an anomaly.

Another example: Dad comes home early from work one Friday afternoon to take the family to the movies. In his rush to get home, he doesn't notice the policeman hiding behind the billboard along the side of the road until it's too late. The policeman gives him a speeding ticket.

When dad gets home, he slams the door shut and says: "Those damn cops are out to get you." Billy, who is 7, overhears his father's remark. In that instant, Billy acquires a new belief: "You can't trust cops." From that moment on, Billy looks for evidence to validate this belief. Any time he sees or hears about police behaving badly, he reinforces his belief.

Age 7 seems to be the magic age between gullibility and discernment.

A comic summed it up best. She said when she came down for breakfast on the day she turned 7, her mom said: "Happy birthday, sweetheart, you've reached the age of reason." She repeated to her mother, "age of reason?" Her mother told her: "We are Catholics and we believe that everything you do wrong before the age of 7 doesn't get counted against your mortal soul. But everything you do wrong after 7 does." The punch line of the joke: "Why didn't you tell me this information when I was 6, when I could have really used it?"

Beliefs and salespeople

Because we get our beliefs by age 7, the thought process we used to create them was quite simple. When we articulate a belief, we tend to use a simple sentence structure as well. For instance, to uncover beliefs about salespeople, I ask my workshop participants to finish this sentence: "Salespeople are _____."

When someone says something positive, like "salespeople are driven," I record that response on a flipchart with a green pen. When someone else in the audience responds with a negative attribute, like "salespeople are sleazy," I use a red pen. Within minutes, the list of negative beliefs in red is three times larger than the list in green.

After a while, one of the salespeople in the audience will yell out: "That's not us! We would never take advantage of somebody just to get a sale." That may be true, but our cultural views of selling and salespeople are mostly negative.

It does not matter how much a salesperson wants to be a sales superstar. Their beliefs about selling, along with their self-worth, determine the results they achieve. Remember, beliefs always trump desires.

The impact of beliefs on a sales team

I was working with a sales team in Silicon Valley. Alan, the vice president for worldwide sales, said: "We talk a good game, but my salespeople cave in on price all the time."

This $40-million company competes with giants like Intel and Motorola. When I started interviewing members of the sales team, it became apparent that they didn't trust other departments in the company. I extended the interviews to the support, marketing, administration, and finance departments. Trust was lacking throughout the organization.

In a two-day retreat with key personnel from all departments, we uncovered the beliefs ("they never come through", "they put their goals ahead of our department", and "they are unhelpful on purpose) that were driving this lack of trust. Using techniques from neuroscience, we transformed the beliefs of the participants.

During follow-up interviews I conducted three months after the retreat, the salespeople reported substantial change in their behavior and the attitudes of people in the other departments. One salesperson said: "In the past when we came back from a customer who needed something customized, I would hear 'we can't do that.' Now the first thing I hear is 'how do we make that happen?' This shift in behavior has changed our entire organization."

Alan reported that the new level of trust had increased deal size by 200 percent.

Chapter Six

THE MODEL OF THE WORLD

As discussed in the first chapter, your brain accounts for 2 percent of your body mass and uses 25 percent of your body's energy. This sounds like a lot but it turns out it's not, because your brain's number-one responsibility is to keep you alive. To do that, it needs to ensure that you have enough energy to "fight like hell" or "run like hell" when danger appears – the "fight or flight" response.

To conserve energy your brain creates a model of how the world works. This allows you to make decisions with minimal thinking. The advantage of such a model is that you make decisions faster. The disadvantage is that you only accept things that already exist in the model.

When you ask a person to do something that does not exist in their model, they will be resistant to taking the actions necessary to accomplish it – because they don't believe they can or that it's even possible.

We all have friends, for instance, who could accomplish so much more in their lives – like writing a book or starting a business. When we suggest to them that they could write a book they simply can't imagine it. They might say that sounds like a great idea, but they won't take the first action to make it a reality. Why? Their internal model won't permit them to envision the possibility let alone take the necessary steps to make it a reality.

Take the salesperson who wants to sell more. The sales manager suggests going after Fortune 500 accounts.

To the salesperson, that seems impossible because such a scenario is not in her model. She simply cannot imagine herself in that league. She may attempt to pursue Fortune 500 business, perhaps asking for leads or assembling a list of targets. But internally, her brain is saying: "You are not sophisticated enough to do business with a Fortune 500 company." These negative thoughts will sabotage her efforts.

Organizations as a whole also have models of the world that shape their actions. This is why it is so difficult for them to change directions.

Models are also self-fulfilling prophecies. Here's a case in point: When Intel's American managers visited the company's research facility in Israel, they'd walk by a conference room and typically see managers in a meeting screaming at each other. They would turn to their Israeli hosts and ask if a call to Security should be made. Not necessary, the Israelis would say. It was just a typical meeting. Israelis have a different model of the world compared to their American counterparts. In their world view they are intense and will do whatever it takes to get their point across.

Gordon Moore, one of Intel's founders, predicted that computing power would double every 18 months. Intel's model of the world, therefore, recognized that the speed of its processor must increase. This would ensure the fulfillment of "Moore's Law."

The Israeli research scientists, however, knew that increasing the speed of the chip would eventually lead to excessive amounts of

generated heat, which would melt the chip and render it useless. They suggested using dual-core technology. This two-processor structure would increase power, yet keep the speed of the chip at a level that would not overheat the chip.

For Intel – a company made up of scientists and engineers- the data should have trumped their model of the world. However, the company's leadership held on to their belief that increasing chip speed was the only way to double power.

After years of badgering, the Israelis finally persuaded Intel's management team to switch over to dual-core processing. Intel went from low profitability and a low stock price to once again dominating the microprocessor industry. The new technology sent the company's stock price and profits skyrocketing.

In corporations, the culture is the belief system that employees and management hold. These beliefs determine the corporate perspective (model of the world). This channels employees thinking along a narrow path. The only way to change the path is to first change the beliefs of the management team. Then, it's possible to transform the beliefs of the entire organization. When beliefs change, the model automatically transforms. A new perspective can allow a company to flourish. For the sales department a new model can have huge implications, from increasing market share to creating markets that never existed previously.

Chapter Seven

BELIEFS IN BUSINESS TEAMS

Your beliefs and your model of the world determine your behaviors – what you will do and what you won't do. Behaviors, in turn, determine results. When a salesperson isn't reaching their quota, the sales manager will look at that salesperson's daily activities and suggest trying a new behavior or stop doing an ineffective one.

Most sales managers report that when they give this kind of tactical advice to salespeople it often goes unheeded. Salespeople want to follow directions, but they often fail to do so. Or, they change their behaviors for a short time and then revert back to their old ways.

When I'm doing a presentation to a large group, I sometimes ask the audience if anyone has a 2-year-old at home, or if anyone remembers what it was like when their kids were that age. Hands usually shoot up. Then I ask: "When you tell your 2-year-olds what to do, do they listen?" After the audience erupts in laughter, someone usually says: "Hell, no."

I follow this with similar questions regarding teenagers. "When you tell your teenagers what to do, do they listen?" Of course they don't. It's the same for salespeople. The sales managers in the audience may be the bosses, but that doesn't mean that their salespeople will listen to them.

In America, we spend $7.8 billion on sales training each year. ES Research, a company that measures the results of sales training, has found that the training wears off after 80 days.

Just telling salespeople what to do differently does not work, unless you address the underlying beliefs that drive their behavior.

During my sessions with business teams and organizations, at some point, I will ask attendees to define what a great team looks like. What are the behaviors that you see team members doing? What are the attitudes that allow them to get exceptional results? The attendees start shouting out attributes and behaviors that they consider to be essential for high-functioning teams.

The list looks something like this:

- Trust
- Great communication
- Clear vision
- Selfless behavior
- Passion
- Tenacity
- Commitment to one another
- Having fun

Then I ask them for the behaviors and attitudes of average teams.

This list looks like this:

- Office politics
- Fear
- Selfishness
- CYA
- Poor communication
- Low trust
- Dislike coming to work

When you have a highly effective team, like the Apple design team, you can accomplish a lot. Members of such teams trust each other, allowing them to develop stronger strategies. These teams have beliefs like:

- Its about the team not me
- The team has my back
- I know others will do their jobs
- It is OK to be honest

Average teams like Blockbuster (went out of business) get less done because there's a lower level of trust among team members – a situation that leads to office politics, which slows the team down. Such teams end up selecting the safest (and sometimes the dumbest) strategies. These teams have beliefs like:

- CYA
- Love the boss's ideas no matter how bad
- Always blame others
- Information is power, so don't share it

Then I ask attendees: "When a company is operating with an average team's mindset, rather than a high-functioning one, how much productivity gets left on the table?" The typical answer is that 40 to 60 percent is lost.

Chapter Eight

LIMITING BELIEFS

We have tens of thousands of beliefs that factor into our levels of success. Most of these beliefs will allow us to do exceptional things. But some of our beliefs get in the way and hinder our best efforts. The best way to uncover a limiting belief is to look for an area of your sales process where you are lackluster.

Where are you pulling your punches – not reaching "4 inches beyond the target?" If there's an area where you want to do better, but no matter how hard you try you still struggle, a limiting belief could be blocking your success.

After one of my presentations, Sarah, a salesperson, set up an appointment to see me. When we met, she told me that she was a multi-level marketing (MLM) professional. Sarah was earning $125,000 a year, which means that she knows what she's doing because most people in the MLM industry never reach that level of success. Sarah had been stuck at this level for years.

I asked her to describe a particular time when she thought about why she was not doing better. She mentioned that just a few days before she was in her office thinking about that very thing. I asked her to re-live that moment in her mind, to see what she saw back then and hear what she had heard then.

(When you do those two things, you get to re-experience what you were feeling at the time.)

"What are you feeling now?" I asked.

"I felt this tightness in my chest."

I used a tool from neuroscience to link this feeling to Sarah's unconscious mind. The unconscious mind records everything and this tool allowed her to go back to the original time she had this exact feeling. Instantly, she was transported back in time to an event that happened when she was just 5 years old.

Her dad had come home from work one Friday afternoon. After the hugs and kisses, her dad reached into his back pocket to retrieve his weekly paycheck and discovered he had lost it on the way home. He started to cry. This was the only time she'd ever seen her dad cry. In that instant, she created a belief around money and her father. Beliefs get created in crisis situations when emotions are turned way up high. This event fit the bill.

What we uncovered in that session was that Sarah created a belief that she must honor her father. She was violating this belief by earning $125,000, while her father had never earned more than $80,000 in his best year. This belief was sabotaging her efforts to break through her financial barrier. Using a neuroscience tool, we identified the limiting belief and transformed it into a positive one.

The intention behind the belief

The key to changing a belief is to identify the positive intention of the old limiting belief. In this case, it was "honoring her father."

This positive intention had locked in the limiting belief that was causing so much frustration. No matter how hard she tried, she could not overcome this barrier. I helped her to develop a new belief that shared the same positive intention: "How well you do is a testament to your father's greatness."

She recognized that the old belief was creating frustration and anxiety (lots of pain). The new belief would allow her to achieve her dreams and bring happiness and pleasure into her life. The human mind automatically adopts pleasure over pain as long as the belief you are changing stays true to the positive intention.

A couple of weeks later Sarah called and said: "I'm not sure what you did, but my sales are taking off."

I did not teach Sarah how to sell more. I only showed her how to transform a limiting belief into an empowering one. With this new mindset, she operates at a higher, more effective level, which allows her to achieve dramatically better results.

Chapter Nine

HOT-WIRED PROCESSES

Another factor that causes salespeople to get stuck is something I call hot-wiring. During a keynote speech when I reach this point, I stop presenting and walk out into the audience and find a female attendee. I go over to her and put out my hand for her to shake. This is the trigger for her to shake my hand. "I don't think we've met, I'm Umar," I say. The woman reaches out and shakes my hand. (Now, the audience is thinking: "Dude, date on your own time.")

When I get back to the stage I explain that there are three parts that make up a human brain. The reptile brain keeps us safe and alive. The limbic brain is all about emotions. And, the neocortex is all about language, strategy and higher-level thinking.

When I stuck out my hand it triggered Kelly's reptile brain. She had to decide if it would be safe to shake my hand – because, quite literally, by doing so, Kelly would be allowing me (a stranger) to grab hold of her body. Kelly took my hand without consciously being aware that her reptile brain made a decision it was safe for her to do so.

Kelly then had to decide how firmly she would shake my hand. Not firm enough and I would think she's a wimp. Too firm and I would think I'm a wimp. If Kelly doesn't shake my hand long enough, I would think she's stuck up. And, if she shakes my hand a half-second longer than she should, I'm going to think she is flirting with me. All of these complex decisions happen outside of Kelly's conscious awareness. She was only aware of my hand (the trigger).

The human brain is always trying to conserve energy. It hot-wires processes that allow complex actions to take place without a lot of thinking (wasted energy).

Here's another example.

Brian is a financial advisor who came to see me because he was struggling in his sales career. He said he should have quit three months ago because he was starving. He had not been making cold calls and as a result, he was getting few appointments and not enough sales.

He knew that cold calling is the fastest way to get more appointments and increase sales. With that in mind, he opted to take a number of courses on effective cold calling. Yet, no matter how much he wanted to succeed, he felt extremely uncomfortable when it came time to make calls. He'd do anything other than picking up the phone.

Using neuroscience techniques, I was able to get Brian to look at what was really going on in his unconscious mind. Each time Brian saw his office phone his mind would launch a hot-wired process that blocked him from success. Looking at the phone was the trigger (just like the handshake in the earlier example) that caused Brian to say to himself: "I'm no good at this." Then, he'd visualize a busy executive becoming angry after being interrupted by his call. Brian allowed that inner dialogue and image to create self-anxiety. In fact, the uncomfortable feelings would intensify until the last thing Brian wanted to do was to pick up the phone.

My 12 years of experience in working with people has taught me that we are not thinking creatures that feel. We are feeling creatures that think. Another way to look at it is that feelings involve a deeper process than thinking. It's why just wishing something to change doesn't work.

The trick to changing a hot-wired process is to take the same trigger that activates the problem and use it to launch a new process that delivers better results. To build this new process, it's necessary to use emotions and feelings, not thinking, to create change.

The first thing I asked Brian was to think about a time when he felt deeply curious. Brian thought for a moment and then remembered that when he was 7 years old, he discovered where his mother hid his Christmas present. He couldn't open the wrapping, but he did shake the package and try to smell it. He was extremely curious to figure out what was in that package. We used that feeling of deep curiosity to be the first step in the new hot-wired process we were building.

Then I asked Brian to think of a particular time when he was decisive. He said, "When I decided to run my first marathon I felt total decisiveness. We set it aside to use later in the process.

Finally, I asked Brian to think of a time when he had a burning desire. Brian told me that when he graduated from college, he had no business buying a new car. But nothing in the world was going to stop him because that new car was a symbol of his arrival as a business professional.

We created a new neural pathway for Brian that would be triggered by looking at a phone. It would cause Brian to feel deep curiosity for an instant, leading him to imagine all the possibilities of using the phone. Then he'd feel decisiveness, for just an instant, forcing him to choose one of those possibilities. And, an instant or two later, he'd have a burning desire to take action on his decision, as if it were the most important task in the world.

Brian's brain now had two neural pathways that would be triggered by looking at a phone. The first one led him to berate himself while creating negative images, which forced him to feel dreadful – and lots of pain.

The second pathway caused him to feel deep curiosity, then decisiveness, and then a burning desire to take action. This pathway led to more appointments and sales – and more pleasure.

As previously mentioned, the human brain will always pick pleasure over pain. Within an hour and a half, we re-wired Brian's thinking. It was apparent that something changed. Brian looked happier and more relaxed than he did when he came in. I told Brian to try making his calls every day for the following week and report back to me. A week later, Brian came in for his appointment and said he had effortlessly made all his calls that week.

We literally have thousands of hot-wired processes that allow us to quickly accomplish things.

For instance, there's a selection process that you use for picking out clothes to wear or items on a restaurant menu. However, there are other hot-wired processes that get in our way. Procrastination is an excellent example of a limiting hotwired process.

Chapter Ten

INNER CONFLICTS

Ever wonder what stops a salesperson who knows in her heart that she can be a great salesperson? It is frustrating having the desire but not being able to attain the results.

One possibility is having an inner conflict. This happens when on one hand, she is confident of being a great salesperson. On the other hand, she feels inadequate in some way. "If only I had a better education, or I was better looking", she tells himself. This inner conflict creates a lot of stress, doubt and anxiety that leads to failure.

One way to identify if a person has inner conflict is to watch their body language. When one part of their psyche is talking (I know I can do X), they use a strong tone of voice and one of their hands uses strong gestures as they talk. When the conflicted part of their psyche (I'm not good enough) talks it uses a weaker tone of voice and the other hand uses weaker hand gestures.

A few years ago, Jill came to see me. Jill is chief salesperson for a small five-person company that sells specialty products. She complained that she would meet people at networking events, and then when she called to set up appointments they refused. "As soon as I hang up the phone," she said, "I know what I should've said." Interesting: she knew what to say, but the words failed her when it counted. This lack of appointments had a catastrophic effect on her sales.

In our session, I noticed when Jill was telling me, "I know I can be great at sales", she used a strong voice and talked with her left hand using strong gestures.

Then she would switch to her right hand and say in a weak voice: "I don't have any formal sales training." This contrast immediately revealed an inner conflict. Using a tool from neuroscience, we were able to resolve the conflict in one session.

You can find out how to resolve inner-conflicts in my advanced neuroscience online training. Visit NoLimitsSelling.com to get more information.

We had our session late one Friday afternoon. I told her, "When you get to work Monday, I want you to call up some of the people you met networking this week and ask for an appointment." She agreed.

On Monday, she reported that with the very first call she made, she got an appointment. It was such a rare thing that she did a dance to celebrate. She made five appointments that day and 17 appointments in total that week.

When she came back the following week Jill said: "It's like the right words fell out of my mouth." I didn't teach her a thing about selling. I just helped her resolve the inner conflict.

We've all heard people say something like this: "A part of me wants to buy this house, but another part of me doesn't think I can afford it." We often think this is just a phrase we're using. In reality, the language we use illuminates the struggle that's going on inside our minds. This type of conflict is kryptonite for salespeople.

Chapter Eleven

COMMUNICATION MASTERY

A core skill for a leader, as we will see, is the ability to communicate clearly and powerfully. These pointers can enhance your ability to communicate with your team.

It turns out that language is a high-level function for the human brain. At a basic level, humans acquire and process information in coordination with their senses, or modalities. The modalities are:

- Visual - what we see (still images and video)
- Auditory - what we hear (mono and surround sound)
- Kinesthetic - what we can physically touch and the emotions we feel
- Olfactory - what we smell
- Gustatory - what we taste

All humans have a preferred mode of communication. The way to uncover someone's preferred modality is to listen to the words that individual uses. Are the words primarily visual, auditory, kinesthetic, olfactory or gustatory? Uncovering preferred modalities allows you to communicate at a deeper level, while also enhancing levels of trust.

Visual people

Some people talk in pictures. They might use words like – I can see that clearly, or they may say: "I am looking for the big picture or the future looks really bright." These people are visual. Use visual words and they will understand what you are saying much faster. In fact, when you start using visual terms like – "I can see clearly" – you'll notice they respond by nodding their heads with micro-movements that indicate unconscious rapport.

Auditory people

These people are all about sound. They will say things like: being on "the right frequency," or "sounds good to me," and "that rings a bell." When you interact with them, use auditory language and you will win them over. Look for head-nodding here, as well.

Kinesthetic people

These people talk in feelings and use phrases like: "I'm looking for something that has a hard impact," or "a solution I can grasp on to." When you interact with them, use kinesthetic words to reach a deeper connection. Once again, look for head-nodding as a sign of trust for you.

Mastering the use of modalities in your language allows you to take your communications to levels that foster unwavering trust.

As a result, people begin to offer information they'd otherwise have been reluctant to share. This enhanced level of communication also makes people more comfortable. They are apt to become more engaged. And, team engagement leads to improved team outcomes.

Communication Breakdown

Albert Mehrabian, a psychology professor at UCLA, discovered that 7 percent of communication comes through the words we use, 38 percent through the tonality of our voice, and a whopping 55 percent from our body language.

To be a master communicator, you need to master the versatility of your voice. The human voice has many aspects to it, including:

- Volume
- Speed of speech
- Cadence
- Tonality

The concept I'm about to share with you is based on the fact that people tend to befriend people like themselves.

Consider your own friends. They are like you in many ways. For example, close friends tend to talk in the same manner. They use similar volume, speed and cadence in their conversations. Our unconscious mind equates these similarities with trust because they are indicative of relationships among friends.

With regard to your team, some members may speak rapidly, others more slowly. Some may have loud voices, others have soft voices. Some may enunciate every syllable, others will use a sing-song cadence. To establish a deep connection with every team member, match vocal attributes as you speak to each person.

Using the same volume, speed and cadence with team members forges a bond of trust that allows them to let their guard down and share what they're really thinking. This skill increases the level of trust your followers have in you, which in turn, allows you to lead them to new levels of excellence.

Body language

In addition to speaking in the same manner, it also turns out that friends use the same body language with each other during their conversations.

Remember that UCLA's Albert Mehrabian demonstrated how body language accounts for some 55 percent of our communication. When you match another person's body language, it is a powerful way to quickly establish bonds of trust. Most people do this unconsciously with their trusted friends.

In fact, as you watch two close friends engaged in conversation, you'll see an intricate ballet of body movement. The two might be seated in a manner that reflects the same body posture. As one person re-crosses her legs, right over left, the friend follows that lead a few seconds later and changes position to maintain the rapport.

The brain is hotwired to match a friend's body language because it feels good and re-enforces trust. If another person is matching our body language, our brain tells us to trust this person. Just like magic, you have a new friend.

Have you ever met a stranger and felt an instant connection? It was like this person knew you intimately and you felt an immediate sense of trust. You might have even said: "It's like I've known you all of my life!" For all you know, that stranger might have been a CIA operative trained to in body language to break down your defenses. (You didn't divulge any state secrets or offer up your ATM access code, did you? If so, call your bank and change your PIN code immediately.)

The two main components for building rapport through body language are body-positioning and gesture-matching.

It is essential to match or mirror another person's body language. If that person is sitting with arms folded (left arm over right), do the same, or sit as if you are a mirror image with your right arm over the left. Matching and mirroring are both effective ways to forge connections.

If the person is sitting with head tilted to one side, or standing with more weight on the left leg, do the same. Basically, match or mirror whatever the other person is doing.

Keep in mind that you are not trying to mock another person. You are showing respect by making an effort to build rapport. If you convey disrespect, that person will pick up your negative vibe in seconds and feel distrust for you.

You can also match the other person's gestures. If someone raises a left hand about 4 feet above the ground and says: "We have to reach a higher level of excellence," you respond with the same gesture and comment as you talk about excellence.

Later in the conversation, you might hold up your left hand 4 feet in the air and say: "If I get this straight, your goal is to reach this level of excellence. Is that right?" You will see the other person nod their head with body language that says: "Yes, you really get me."

In a team setting you can't match everyone's body language at the same time. You only have to match the body language and gestures of the person you are connecting to at that moment. The trust generated opens up the conversation so people stop saying only what they think you want to hear. You get to the truth, so you can solve the "real" problem.

Most people use gestures unconsciously. One person might favor small gestures, while another prefers grand, sweeping gestures, and yet another may not use gestures at all.

If you are not one to incorporate big gestures into your conversations, try using a smaller-scale version of the gesture that the person you are talking with is using. It works wonders. If you try matching the other person's big gestures and it makes you feel uncomfortable, the other person will pick that up. Match the other person in a way that makes you feel more true to your style. Paying attention to gestures always yields large dividends because it really amps up the trust.

Attending

Attending is a fancy way of saying that you are concerned about acknowledging others. When people speak, I nod as my way of encouraging them to continue. I do not speak while people are thinking and sharing ideas, but I use short phrases like "Go on" or "Aha" as a way of saying please continue, I'm interested in what you are saying. You can also get your body language into the attending process by looking at them expectantly. You will be surprised at how much more information people will share with this simple form of encouragement.

And finally, when people begin to offer ideas, praise them by saying: "Yeah! That's a really good idea." It encourages them to go on and it also makes other group members want to contribute to the conversation.

If someone gives you a quizzical look, or an "I-got-things-I-want-to-share" look, say: "It appears that you've got some ideas to share."

This encourages people to start sharing things that they were reluctant to share a moment ago. Attending creates a safe environment that makes people feel more comfortable, allowing them to participate in a more engaged manner.

Once you start mastering these simple communication skills, you take your leadership to elevated levels. Additionally, as you use these skills, you are modeling the behaviors you want your team members to adopt. As team members use this subtle form of communication, it also enhances the level of trust in your organization.

Chapter Twelve

ANCHORING EXCELLENCE

Have you ever had the experience of listening to a song on the radio and being transported back to a pleasant memory from the distant past? This is not just recalling the event. It's a much richer experience that taps into the emotion of that experience. According to neuroscientists, an event has two associated components: emotions and data (visuals, sounds, and thoughts). Most events do not have heightened emotions so the brain codes these experiences as average.

For example making a toast would be an average, mundane event involving limited or no emotions. It would be difficult to remember such an event even a few hours later. Basically, it's a non-event.

When we experience a highly emotional event, however, our brains code this experience as exceptional. The emotions could have been positive or negative. Our brains care only about the intensity of the emotion. These events get recorded in high-definition, so all aspects – even those below the level of conscious awareness get recorded.

For example, if a teenager was having a highly enjoyable party with her friends at the beach, her brain would pay attention to all her senses. The song playing in the background would forever be linked to that experience at the beach. Even decades later, just hearing that song would instantly transport her back to that experience. She would not just be remembering the event; she would re-live it in all of its richness. This is an unconscious human ability that we all possess. In NLP, this process is known as anchoring.

NLP founders have deconstructed how a brain links a stimulus (like a song) to the rich emotions contained in a past experience. This NLP process lets you instantly access any emotion that you have experienced in the past.

Think about it: if you were about to research something that held no interest for you, how well do you think you'd accomplish the task? Not well, right?

What if you had the ability to become highly curious before starting that research? Your curiosity would allow you to dig deeper and to be more tenacious in your efforts. You would deliver better results! NLP allows anyone to access curiosity instantly and so much more.

Imagine you're about to do the biggest deal of your career and negative thoughts start to sabotage your efforts. What if you could flip a mental switch and instantly feel confident and powerful. These positive emotions would allow you to easily close that deal!

Learning how to anchor

Step 1: Decide what you want to use as a trigger to access the target emotion. The trigger could be physical, like pressing the fourth knuckle on your right hand. It could be auditory – when you hear a particular sound or word. The trigger could also be visual one. For instance, just looking at your phone would trigger an insatiable desire to pick it up and start making calls.

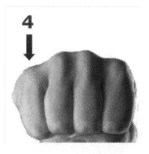

Step 2: Decide what target emotion you want to access. If you want to have the feeling of being highly confident, recall a particular time when you had that feeling. You may have had that feeling for an hour or for a few only seconds. It doesn't matter how long you felt it. The critical consideration is that the target emotion was intense.

Let's say you want to access the feeling of being confident and powerful. This feeling, or mindset, would be extremely useful in any sales situation. It would allow you to close a deal on your very next sales appointment.

Step 3: To access the target feeling, remember a particular time you felt it intensely. Go back to that memory and see what you saw back then. Hear what you heard back then. This forces your body to experience the target feeling instantly. You only have to notice where in your body you feel that emotion.

Step 4: Increase the intensity of that feeling by imagining a volume knob. Just turn that imaginary knob and increase the intensity of the emotion.

When you have the emotion amped-up, move to the next step. This technique can increase the intensity of the emotion to a higher level than the original experience.

Step 5: Again, see what you saw when you felt that emotion. Hear what you heard back then and notice the intensity of the target emotion. Just press the fourth knuckle of your left hand firmly. This creates a link between your knuckle and that emotion.

Step 6: Repeat steps 4 and 5 several times to train your neurology to reinforce the anchor. This ensures that pressing the trigger instantly unleashes that emotion.

Congratulations, you now have the ability to decide how you want to feel in any situation. You can create several anchors allowing you to access the following emotions:

Patience: Useful when dealing with a challenging client, your boss or a spouse in crisis.

Curiosity - Useful when you're collecting information from a prospect before you go in for the close.

Powerful - Useful when you're negotiating a higher price than your competitors.

The possibilities are endless. All you have to do is think about what emotion would serve you best in a particular situation. Find a past memory when you experienced the desired emotion and anchor it.

Chapter Thirteen

GETTING UNSTUCK

In Chapter 12 you learned how to anchor a feeling that you could trigger at will. This technique can change the quality of your life in immeasurable ways. The only issue is that you have to remember to use the trigger for it to work. When you're doing a stressful task, you may not remember to use the trigger.

In this chapter you'll learn how to use a negative feeling to trigger an empowering one. In challenging situations, negative emotions arise instantly. The beauty of this enhanced technique is that as soon as your brain registers a negative feeling, it automatically triggers the empowering one. You don't have to do anything, it just happens.

The sales breakthrough builds upon the anchoring technique. During this process, we will manually anchor two emotions. The first emotion is the uncomfortable feeling that gets in the way of you doing a particular task well. The second is the positive emotion that will empower you to successfully and effortlessly complete that task.

The final step of the process uses the negative emotion that hindered you in the past to automatically trigger the positive emotion that will propel you to success.

The Getting Unstuck: Part 1 – Anchor negative emotion

Step 1: Choose knuckle one on your non-dominant hand as the trigger for the unwanted emotion.

Step 2: Think of a specific time when you went to do a particular task and felt that negative feeling. This is the emotion that we want to capture.

Step 3: Go back to that event in your mind and see what you saw back then. Hear what you heard back then, and notice where in your body you feel that negative emotion.

Step 4: Since this is a negative emotion there is no need to increase its intensity. We're only looking to use this negative emotion to trigger the desired emotion. As soon as you feel the uncomfortable feeling, press knuckle one firmly to anchor it.

Step 5: Now, think of something totally different for a moment so you can let go of the negative emotion. This is like eating sorbet between dinner courses in order to cleanse your palate before the next bite.

Step 6: Press knuckle one and notice how quickly that uncomfortable feeling flows into your body. If this happens, move on to Part 2. Otherwise, repeat Steps 3 to 6 until the anchor works.

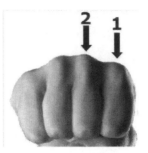

The Getting Unstuck: Part 2 – Anchoring positive emotion

Step 1: Choose a second knuckle (knuckle two) on your non-dominant hand as the trigger for the desired emotion (the feeling that would allow you to effortlessly complete that task).

Step 2: Think of a particular time when you felt the desired feeling intensely and go back to that event in your mind.

Step 3: See what you saw back then. Hear what you heard back then and notice where in your body you feel the desired emotion.

Step 4: Use the imaginary volume knob and start increasing the intensity of the positive feeling. The stronger you make this feeling; the more useful it is for you. (What's better: feeling somewhat confident or feeling totally confident?)

Step 5: Press knuckle two firmly while you're seeing what you saw back then, hearing what you heard back then and feeling this intense emotion. This will link knuckle two to the positive emotion.

Step 6: Repeat steps 4 and 5 several times to forever link knuckle two to the desired emotion.

Step 7: Think of something totally different so you can test the link and see how quickly the feeling comes flooding back into your body.

Step 8: Press knuckle two and notice how quickly this feeling comes back. If it happens quickly and powerfully, you're ready to move on to Part 3 of the process. If not, repeat steps 4 to 8 until you are successful.

Now that we have the negative feeling and the positive feeling anchored to your knuckles, we're ready to move on to the final step.

The Getting Unstuck: Part 3 – Rewiring your brain

Step 1: Press knuckle one to trigger the negative emotion. The instant you feel it, move on to step 2.

Step 2: While holding onto knuckle one, press knuckle two to trigger the positive emotion. The instant you feel the positive emotion release knuckle one so the negative emotion is no more.

Step 3: Continue pressing knuckle two so that you are only feeling the positive emotion. The longer you hold the second knuckle, the stronger the feeling gets.

Step 4: Release the second knuckle.

Step 5: Repeat Steps 1 to 4 several times to train your brain that any time you feel the uncomfortable feeling it automatically triggers the powerful desired feeling.

Step 6: Test it - think about doing the challenging task now and notice how much more confident you are in successfully completing it.

Chapter Fourteen

PSYCHO-GEOGRAPHY

Anchoring is the linking of a feeling to an object, physical location, sound, sight or aroma. For example, Tommy was so excited that he could not get to sleep the night before his trip to the planetarium. He was 7-years-old and literally vibrating with excitement when he took his seat in the audience at the planetarium the next day.

Thirty years later, Tommy returned to the planetarium for an American Cancer Society fundraising event. The instant he saw the planetarium, he felt the same excitement he had experienced during his childhood visit. Tommy's mind had unconsciously linked the planetarium with a sense of excitement. Even after 30 years, the anchor remained strong.

Think about it: Seeing the planetarium instantly changed Tommy's brain chemistry. We all inherently have the capacity for anchoring.

Here's another example: Sandra, walking down Main Street, notices an enticing aroma emanating from a bakery. The aroma instantly transports Sandra back to her grandmother's kitchen, when she was 4-years-old. The anchoring is so strong she can see every detail of that memory, as if she is re-living it. She can taste the cookies her grandmother has just baked. And, she experiences the deep feeling of being loved. All of this happens in a moment, right then and there on the street.

With the realization that anchoring is a natural human experience – which all of us can experience at an unconscious level – I will show you how to create an anchor, intentionally.

I've coined a new term: "psycho-geography." This term comes into play when a feeling is anchored specifically to a physical location. The feeling can be linked to a physical structure, as in the example of Tommy's experience. It can even be linked to a spot on the floor. Once a feeling is anchored, just stepping on that spot will trigger the associated feeling.

"Anchors Aweigh!"

Just imagine having the ability to decide how you want to feel at any given time. Use the following steps to create an anchor on the floor:

Anchoring Revisited

Anchoring is the linking of a feeling to an object, physical location, sound, sight or aroma. For example, Tommy was so excited that he could not get to sleep the night before his trip to the planetarium. He was 7-years-old and literally vibrating with excitement when he took his seat in the audience at the planetarium the next day.

Thirty years later, Tommy returned to the planetarium for an American Cancer Society fundraising event. The instant he saw the planetarium, he felt the same excitement he had experienced during his childhood visit. Tommy's mind had unconsciously linked the planetarium with a sense of excitement. Even after 30 years, the anchor remained strong.

Think about it: Seeing the planetarium instantly changed Tommy's brain chemistry. We all inherently have the capacity for anchoring.

Here's another example: Sandra, walking down Main Street, notices an enticing aroma emanating from a bakery. The aroma instantly transports Sandra back to her grandmother's kitchen, when she was 4-years-old. The anchoring is so strong she can see every detail of that memory, as if she is re-living it. She can taste the cookies her grandmother has just baked. And, she experiences the deep feeling of being loved. All of this happens in a moment, right then and there on the street.

With the realization that anchoring is a natural human experience – which all of us can experience at an unconscious level – I will show you how to create an anchor, intentionally.

I've coined a new term: "psycho-geography." This term comes into play when a feeling is anchored specifically to a physical location. The feeling can be linked to a physical structure, as in the example of Tommy's experience. It can even be linked to a spot on the floor. Once a feeling is anchored, just stepping on that spot will trigger the associated feeling.

"Anchors Aweigh!"

Just imagine having the ability to decide how you want to feel at any given time. Use the following steps to create an anchor on the floor:

1) What do you want to feel?

Decide what emotion would serve you best in this situation. You could pick something fun like happiness or invincibility. Think of a time from your past when you had such a feeling. Go back to that memory and see what you saw then. This engages the visual center of your brain, making the event come alive.

2) Hear what you heard

Now, hear what you heard during that past event. This engages the auditory center of your brain, making the event even more real.

Seeing and hearing the past event compels your brain to re-live the event fully, so you experience the exact feeling you had then. Wait, it gets even better!

3) Pump-up the volume

With Anchoring, you can also intensify the target feeling to a level that's more powerful than the original experience. To do this, imagine you have a volume knob that controls the intensity of the feeling. All you have to do is to determine which way – clockwise or counter-clockwise – turns the feel up. Just reach out, grab the knob and intensify the feeling. Make the feeling really strong.

4) Creating a "psycho-geography" anchor

At this point, you will fully experience the feeling you are trying to anchor. Select a spot on the floor that you want to anchor to the feeling. Step on that exact spot and simply let all of the feeling flow from your body, through your feet into the floor. Don't worry, you won't lose the feeling. It is waiting for you to reclaim it at that very spot.

Take a step back from the target spot, leaving the feeling there. Notice that your target feeling is gone, and you are feeling normal.

Now, you only have to test the target anchor on the floor. Step back on the anchor spot and notice how quickly the feelings come flooding back into your body.

Anchoring allows you to decide how you want to feel in any situation. Anchoring can change your life.

NOTE: You could anchor a feeling of intense happiness on your front doormat. This would ensure that no matter how bad your workday was, you would be instantly happy every time you stepped on the doormat. Unfortunately, the family dog may feel neglected because you'd never come home mad enough to kick it.

Chapter Fifteen

THE DISNEY TECHNIQUE

Walt Disney changed the world with his creativity, drive and leadership. He built empires out of swamps and created worlds where characters like Mary Poppins could fly. His first step was to create a vision of what the future looked like. Then he made his vision a reality.

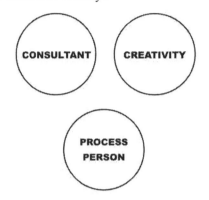

Robert Dilts studied this technique. He used Neuro-Linguistic Programming (NLP) to decode how Disney tapped into his incredible creativity. In this section, you will learn how to use the Disney technique to create fantastic new worlds and ideas.

There are three parts to the creative process in the Disney technique:

Creativity – to come up with insanely great ideas

Consulting – to make the ideas better and more strategic

Process – to build a step-by-step plan to make the creation a reality

The underlying technology that we are going to use is Anchoring (NeuroBooster 1).

You will anchor the feelings of creativity, consultant and process person in three individual spots on the floor.

Spot One – Creativity

1) Think creative

Think of a time from your past when you felt highly creative. It could have been yesterday or it could have been when you were 9-years-old, planning an adventure with your friends. It does not matter which memory you use, just that you felt highly creative at the time.

Go back to that memory, using your mind's eye, and see what you saw then. You will start to feel creative and notice where (chest, head, etc) in your body you feel it.

2) Hear it

Now, hear what you heard back then when you felt highly creative. This will make the creative feeling grow stronger.

3) Pump-up the volume

Imagine you have a volume knob that controls the intensity of that creative feeling. Now, turn up the creative feeling so that your entire body is filled with it. The stronger you make the feeling, the easier it is to be creative.

4) Step into the creativity spot

Select a spot on the floor that you want to anchor to creativity. Step on to the exact spot and simply let all of the feeling flow from your body, through your feet into that spot. Now, step away from the spot, leaving all of the feeling of creativity there.

Don't worry, you won't lose the feeling. It will be waiting for you to pick it up again. Notice that you feeling normal, again.

Test that it worked!

Step back onto the creativity spot and notice how quickly the feelings of creativity come flooding back into your body.

Congratulations! You've just anchored the feeling of creativity to a spot on the floor. Leave the feeling there before you step out because we are going to use this in a moment.

Spot Two – Consultant

1) Think of the best consulting you ever did.

Think of a time from your past when you were a great consultant.

It could have been on a work project in which you actually did business consulting.

It could have been when you were helping your church plan a fundraiser.

Just think of a time when you improved a project. You clearly saw what needed to be done and you changed the plans for the better. It does not matter which memory you use, just that you felt the feeling of "consultant" strongly.

Immerse yourself in that memory, and using your mind's eye, see what you saw back then. You will start to feel the consultant feeling flow in your body.

2) Hear it.

Now, hear what you heard back then when you felt like a highly effective consultant. This will make the feeling get even stronger.

3) Pump up the volume.

Imagine you have a volume knob that controls this feeling. Now, turn up the feeling so that your entire body is experiencing it. Make it really strong.

4) Step into the consultant spot.

Select a spot on the floor near the creativity spot that you are going to use for consultant. Step on the exact spot and simply let all of the feeling of being a consultant flow from your body through your feet into that spot. Now step out of the spot leaving all of the feelings behind.

Test that it worked!

Step back onto the anchor spot and notice how quickly the feelings of being a great consultant come flooding back into your body.

Congratulations! You just anchored the feeling of "Great Consultant." Leave the feeling there, before you step out, because we are going to use this in a moment.

Spot Three – Process-person

1) Think of a time when you easily figured out all the steps needed to complete a project. It could have been on a work project or elsewhere.

Go back to that memory and using your mind's eye, see what you saw back then. You will start to notice the feeling of being a great process-person flow into your body.

2) Hear it.

Now, hear what you heard back then so the feeling gets even stronger.

3) Pump up the volume.

Imagine you have a volume knob that controls this feeling. Now turn up the feeling so your entire body is experiencing it. Make it really strong.

4) Step into the process-person spot.

Select a spot on the floor near the previous two, where you want to anchor process-person to. Step on to the exact spot and simply let all of the feeling flow from your body, through your feet into that spot.

Now, step away from the spot, leaving all of the feeling behind.

Test that it worked!

Step back onto the anchor spot and notice how quickly the feelings of being a great process-person comes flooding back into your body.

Congratulations! You've just anchored the feeling of process person to a spot on the floor. Leave the feeling there before you step away.

Excuse the pun, but now that "the groundwork is done," you are ready to put your "spots" to work to develop an amazing new plan.

The Disney Technique continued...

Think of new project you are trying to launch.

Step into the creativity circle and let the creative feeling flood into your body. You must truly feel the creativity feeling before you move to the next step. This feeling primes your neurology to be programmed for intense creativity.

Now, think of the project that you are working on and notice how your creativity instantly soars.

Let the ideas pour in. Each new idea may launch another 10. If you hear your inner voice say "this is silly," ignore it. Your only job here is to keep up with your inner creative genius.

After five or ten minutes, you will have a clear vision of what the completed project looks like.

Once you have this new, amazing vision of the future, step out of the circle.

Remember to leave the creative feeling behind before you step away from the spot.

Step into the consultant circle and let the feeling of being a great consultant flow into your body. You must experience the consultant feeling before you move on to the next step.

This consulting feeling will let you quickly edit the vision you just created in the creativity spot. The "consultant" will remove some items from your vision and add or strengthen others. The consultant part of you will quickly make the original vision better and more doable.

Remember to leave the consultant feeling behind before you step off the spot.

Step into the process-person spot and let the feeling of being a great process person flow into your body.

I hate to keep repeating myself, but you must feel the feeling strongly before moving to the next step.

This step is so important because the "feeling" changes your brain chemistry and puts you into the most effective process-person mindset.

The "process-person" feeling will quickly let you create a step-by-step plan that makes your vision a reality. The plan helps you address issues, like funding and getting buy-ins, which are necessary for success. These additions may change the vision and take the plan further. This step could take five or ten minutes to do.

When you step away from this spot remember to leave the feeling of process-person behind.

You'll be amazed at how much you have accomplished in a short time. You'll have clarity on what the vision is and a good plan to make it happen.

This is only the end of round one of this process.

The big idea

The magic of the Disney Technique comes from accessing the target feeling for each step of the process.

The feeling alters your brain chemistry so your brain is in optimal mode to execute the job (creativity, consultant or process) at hand.

Round Two

At the end of round one you will have a clear vision and a plan to make it happen. In round two, everything gets better.

To begin, take your plan from round one and step back into the creativity circle. This is useful because your consultant and process-person from round one may have removed some of the creative elements of your original vision. As soon as you step back in the circle, the creativity feeling will flood back into your body. Your creativity soars and makes this plan even better.

Next, leave the creative feeling behind before you step into the consultant's spot. As soon as the consultant feeling comes back, make this new plan better.

Next, leave the consultant feeling behind before you step into the process-person spot. As soon as you feel the process-person feeling, improve the plan.

This is the end of round two. Do a third round of creativity, consultant and process-person, and you will have a well-thought-out plan ready for action.

For most people, the entire process (all three rounds) takes less than one hour. At its conclusion, you have a sophisticated plan ready for implementation.

Chapter Sixteen

THE EINSTEIN PRINCIPLE

In 1905, Albert Einstein published four scientific papers that had a groundbreaking effect on the world of physics. In one, he imagined how the universe would behave if he were traveling through space on a photon at the speed of light. Einstein's imagined perspective in this paper, "On the Electrodynamics of Moving Bodies," led to his special theory of relativity.

"Perspective is worth 80 IQ points." Alan Kay, scientist

A hallmark of the greatest thinkers in history is the ability to see a problem from all sides. Seeing things from different vantage points reveals previously hidden insights. This NeuroBooster shows you how to systematically get a 360-degree perspective in order to design the most elegant response to a problem.

Consider this popular saying: "You can't see the forest for the trees." To me, it means someone is paying too much attention to the details and can't see the importance of the overall situation. Perspective gives you the ability to see the forest, the trees, the ground and the sky. The richer your perspectives, the easier it is to find the best solution.

Indian leader Mahatma Gandhi used perspective masterfully to end 500 years of British occupation of his country in 1947.

He successfully challenged the world's only superpower to back down. It could be argued that the British Empire's position in the world was more substantial than America's current position as a global force. At the time, India was a resource-rich, cash-cow that made England wealthy. The

English had no intention of giving it all up to a man in a loincloth.

To broker a settlement that would liberate his country, Gandhi had to negotiate with four main stakeholders. The Viceroy, Lord Mountbatten, represented the British. Muhammad Ali Jinnah represented the Muslims, and Baldev Singh represented the Sikhs. Jawaharlal Nehru, the fourth stakeholder, represented the Hindus. Nehru became the first prime minister of India following it's independence.

Although the British had overstayed their welcome, they provided stability for 350 million people of numerous cultures and religions who lived in India. All parties feared a civil war. For the British, an even greater fear was the loss of political power once India was reborn.

With such high stakes, it's easy to imagine that tempers were hot and the men at the center of the negotiations were unreasonable.

Gandhi had to guide the process toward independence without alienating any of the participants.

At this time in history everything was in flux. Political winds shifted daily. The future of millions of people had to be weighed with the greater good for the country. And, the five leaders had to contend with their own fears and motivations.

Each proposed action would excite some, and insult or anger others. A single misstep could derail the entire process. Mathematically, there were a million possibilities. Most would lead to failure and a few – perhaps only one – would yield a successful outcome.

Gandhi had to keep all the moving parts straight if he were to successfully navigate his country toward independence. In this section, I will show you how he did it.

Gandhi would imagine he was stepping into Lord Mountbatten's shoes so he could get a clear idea of how Mountbatten would react to one of his proposals. If he imagined he did not get the right response, he would alter the proposal until he was sure it would be accepted.

Then he would take this "winning" proposal and step into Baldev's shoes to see how he would react. Just like Einstein, Gandhi did all this as a thought experiment. He would test and adjust his proposals until he was sure it suited all the participants.

This NeuroBooster teaches you how to do your own thought experiments. I call this technique "The Einstein Principle" because it sounds cool. In the world of NLP it is called Perceptual Positions. This technique allows you to acquire insights as to how others will react to proposals and circumstances.

The Einstein Principle in action

Step One

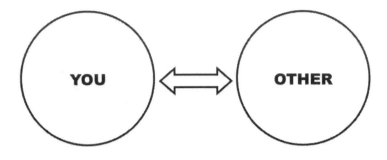

Designate a space on the floor and mark it with a sticky note labeled "YOU." As you may have guessed, this space represents you. Step into the YOU space and get a feel for the proposal or action you are contemplating.

Step Two

Create a space for each of the stakeholders who have an interest in your action or proposal. The stakeholders could be:

- A specific person
- The federal government
- A company
- An environmental group

The main idea is to create a space on the floor that represents the emotions, psyche and agenda of the stakeholder. If the stakeholder is a person, take on that person's demeanor. Literally, take on the same mannerisms, stand and talk as that person would.

If you really get into it, something magical happens. You get insights into that person's true motivations, hopes and concerns. This tool gives you extremely valuable information, which allows you to make better decisions.

Step Three

This will seem weird to some of you, and second nature for others. Trust me and try it. It works. Create a space for the project itself. Just like Einstein imagining the universe from the point of view of a photon of light, this "meta" perspective gives you a deeper understanding of the overall situation.

Step Four

Now step back and forth between all the markers and see the situation from every perspective. Take the insights you derive from one stakeholder to another, so you quickly find a solution that works for all. Note you need to "become that person" when you step into each particular space. You will be surprised how accurately you see that person's perspective.

The Einstein Principle NeuroBooster gives you freedom to focus on individual stakeholder agendas without losing track of the big picture. This allows you to see the forest, the trees and the sky.

NOTE: I have included an actual transcript from a client session online at http://nolimitsselling.com/crazysexy

Chapter Seventeen

THE TESLA EFFECT

Nikola Tesla (1856-1943) was a genius, whose inventions changed the world. He electrified the world when he developed the alternating current (AC) system. He also invented the Tesla coil, which allowed him to transmit radio signals around the globe. (The Tesla Coil looks way cool and has been used as a prop in many sci-fi and horror movies over the years.)

Tesla received more than 300 patents and opted not to apply for patents on many more of his ideas. One of the reasons he was able to create a prolific portfolio of inventions was his ability to quickly create working prototypes.

Tesla would come up with a new idea for a machine. Then he'd build it and run in his mind to see how it worked. If he envisioned a shortcoming, like a bearing wearing out too quickly, he would fix it all in his mind. Basically, he would prototype, enhance and perfect a machine way before he ever built it in the real world. This saved him time, money and resources.

In this section, you will learn how to use the Tesla Effect so you can see the future in your mind before you actually invest time, money and resources.

The Tesla Effect uses floor markers to guide your thinking through the process. We are going to need about 6 feet to 12 feet of space to work in. You will create a NOW marker on one end and a FUTURE marker on the other end. Somewhere in between you will create a SUCCESS marker.

The Tesla Effect

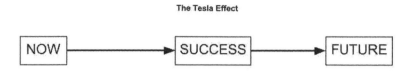

The NOW marker represents your current situation. The SUCCESS marker represents the day you successfully complete the project. The FUTURE marker represents sometime after the successful completion of the project. The FUTURE gives you perspective on the impact of your creation so that you know what needs improving.

Timeline

I borrowed the idea of timeline from Tad James, a prominent Neuro-Linguistic-Programming (NLP) expert who developed this powerful therapeutic technique which helps people overcome traumas. The timeline hinges on looking at your life in chronological order.

I want you to imagine that there is a timeline that starts from the day you were born and ends the day you die. Along this timeline, imagine all the important events in your life from the first day of kindergarten to the day you purchased your first house. Your mind uses a timeline to give structure to your concept of time.

Step one

Use a Post-it note and write the word NOW on it and place it on the floor. Step on that spot and get a really good sense of what you would like to create. Get a good sense of why you are creating this. Get a feel of some of the challenges you will face.

Finally, think about how long it will take you to complete your project.

Step two

Imagine your timeline runs from the NOW spot toward the future. Walking forward (3 feet to 6 feet will do) until you get to the day you complete the project. As you walk out to SUCCESS, get a sense of all the things you had to do to achieve success. These things could include getting a loan, hiring new people, basically anything that led you to a successful outcome. When you arrive at SUCCESS, place the SUCCESS post-it there.

As best you can, fully experience what it will feel like to achieve this great accomplishment. Make this visualization as rich as possible. How are your employees and customers reacting? Are you giving any press interviews? The bottom line here is to see all the positives and negatives of successfully completing the project.

If appropriate see and hear your boss saying, "Great job! You get a big fat raise!" Imagine a letter from an overjoyed customer expressing a desire to order more units. The richer your image, the more you can visualize what success looks and feels like.

Step three

Now it is time to see how this achievement impacts the FUTURE one year out.

Start walking from SUCCESS to where you think a year beyond will be on your timeline (3 feet to 6 feet). As you walk out into the future, get a sense of the impact of your success. When you get a year out, put a Post-it with the word FUTURE on it to mark the spot.

From the FUTURE spot, turn around and look back at what happened in the year after you completed the project. Ask yourself the following questions:

- What could I have done differently?
- Did we maximize the opportunity we generated?
- How could we have gotten faster adoption from our customers?
- Were there features we should have included or excluded?

These questions give you insights on what the initial project goals and parameters should be. You are thinking like Tesla in your effort to find the faulty bearing before you invest money and manpower into the project.

Step four

Walk back to the SUCCESS spot and make the modifications that you envisioned from the FUTURE spot in step four. Get a feel of what new and improved success looks like.

Then look back to the NOW spot and the journey you took to get to SUCCESS. What things do you have to do differently to shorten the time it takes to complete the project? What changes do you have to make to your plans and intentions to ensure you get better results.

Step five

Walk from the SUCCESS spot all the way back to the present (NOW spot), as you get a feel of what works and what needs improving.

When you get to the NOW spot, turn around so you can clearly see the journey ahead of you. On a psychological level, you have "lived it" (at least walked it), allowing you to build a new and improved plan.

The Tesla Effect is an elegant way to prototype new projects in your mind. It helps you to achieve better results and do it faster than ever before.

NOTE: I have included a client session transcript online at http://nolimitsselling.com/crazysexy

Chapter Eighteen

BUILDING A STRONGER TEAM

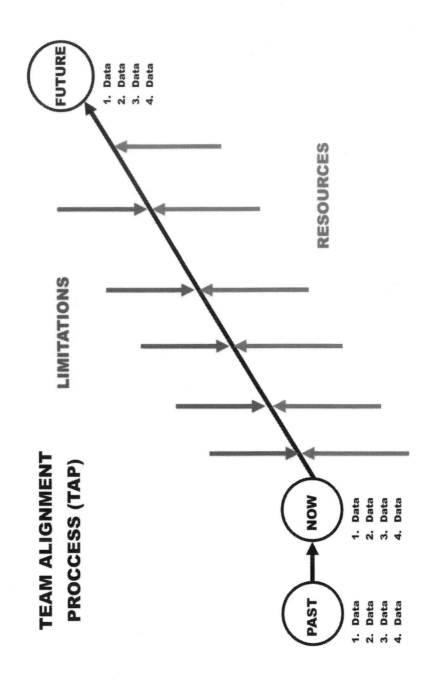

The Team Alignment Process (TAP). This methodology can help your team turn an idea into a highly effective action plan. TAP also ensures that the team will do whatever it takes to successfully execute the plan.

TAP creates a plan with four distinct areas that help to:

1. Clearly define the problem (now, the current state)
2. Get clarity on what the solution (future) looks like
3. Identify limitations that have to be addressed in order to be successful
4. Identify the resources needed for success

The output from TAP elegantly fits on one sheet of paper. If you are working solo, the sheet guides you from start to finish. If you are working with a team, every member gets a copy of the plan on a single sheet of paper, which ensures that everyone is literally on the same page. Everyone on the team has a crystal clear understanding of what needs to be done.

TAP and your team

If the members of your management team were outside consultants, what would they each bill you per hour for their time? Would it be $400 an hour, as much as $1,000 an hour, or more? The bottom line is that each time you gather your team it is costing you a small fortune. If these meetings result in moving your company forward or solving a challenging problem, it is a great investment. Unfortunately, most meetings don't accomplish much and many attendees feel they are wasting time. Remember: A meeting is a terrible thing to waste.

I have delivered keynote speeches in 12 countries so I've had a chance to speak with executives from around the world. One of the complaints that CEOs have shared with me is that they often meet about the same issues month after month, week after week. Mistakenly thinking they have identified the problem and the solution is in the first meeting.

Everybody goes away under that illusion. But, when the team gathers back the following month, they realize that not all of the members are on the same page. Some people have been trying to solve the wrong problem, while others are going about it in a way contrary to what was decided in the original meeting. Getting the entire team to row in the same direction is a critical skill that every great leader has to master.

At other times, emotions get in the way of finding the right solution. If there's a problem, team members think it must have originated in a particular department of the organization. Someone must be at fault. However, people are reluctant to point out the shortcomings of others for fear of being seen as jerks.

The consequences for pointing out failure can range from a genuine thank-you to anger and resentment. In extreme cases, physical violence can result. I once heard of a manager becoming so mad that he punched the Director of Human Resources in the face. This led to the firing of the manager and subsequent legal action. The deeper impact of this unfortunate event is still felt in the organization, all these years later. Managers do not communicate openly because they are afraid of getting punched in the face. For them, it feels safer to keep their mouth shut!

Positive emotions such as passion, creativity, confidence, and urgency are powerful forces for moving the organization and its thinking forward. Negative emotions like selfishness, anger, defensiveness and blame slow or completely stall an organization and its thinking. TAP harnesses the team's positive emotions to deliver better results.

I created TAP to give leaders a simple, elegant solution to think at a higher level so they can become better leaders. TAP also gives leaders a tool to teach their teams to solve problems more elegantly and faster than ever before.

Team members can take this process back to their departments and groups in order to improve the overall thinking process throughout the entire organization.

TAP speeds up the planning process, allowing you to go from zero to solution in half the time.

Once you start using TAP, your meetings become problem-solving sessions that add value to the organization. Your entire team will identify and quantify the problem at hand, and team members can agree that they're on the same page. Then they can identify and quantify what the solution should look like.

They uncover all of the barriers that must be overcome in order to reach the solution. They identify all of the necessary resources to be successful. Then it's a simple matter of agreeing on an action plan to solve the problem. When the team adds timelines and milestones to the action plan it is complete and ready for implementation.

TAP teaches your team to think ahead in order to anticipate and defuse potential problems that could impact your organization. The saving of time, money and resources can be significant. Once TAP starts filtering throughout the organization, you will be surprised how much more effective your entire organization becomes.

TAP is an elegant system that allows you to easily communicate your ideas with your team. It encourages the team to work on a problem with laser-like focus and a sense of urgency. The process gets everyone on the team to be on the same page and going in the same direction, saving countless hours that can be put to better use.

Psychological underpinnings of TAP

Psychology experts describe experiences as being associated or disassociated. An associated experience is one in which you feel all the emotions (good, bad, or ugly) as you go through the event. A disassociated experience is going through an event, but being disconnected from all of your emotions. For most people, life is an associated event because our emotions make life worth living. Yet, disassociation has its advantages, as well, because it allows you to clinically examine a situation without emotions clouding your judgment.

"It's not personal, it's strictly business." Michael Corleone, The Godfather

TAP requires association and disassociation at different points throughout the process. To study, debate and define a problem, it is best to be in an associated mode. This also applies to finding creative solutions in which emotions like excitement, passion and enthusiasm are assets.

To validate the quality of a newly formed solution, a disassociated perspective works best. This approach further ensures that team members do not fall blindly in love with a plan and overlook pitfalls. It also helps the team to maintain a steady, critical focus while developing a realistic action plan.

Step One: Defining NOW

1. Data
2. Data
3. Data
4. Data

Tell the team it is each team member's responsibility to ensure this meeting is a success. They owe it to each other to ask questions and challenge any thoughts or ideas that seem inaccurate or are in need for further clarification. The intention of these questions and push-backs are to get clarity, allowing everyone to be on the same page. The clarity focuses the power and creativity of the team to find a better solution.

Gather your team in your conference room. Go to the whiteboard and draw a circle in the lower-left area of the board and write the word NOW. Tell the team that this represents the current situation, the situation that you are trying to improve. Ask your team: "What does it look like right now? What does it sound like? What does it feel like (tactilely and emotionally)?"

By asking the team – in terms of what they see, hear and feel – you create a filter that takes ambiguity out of the meeting. For example, when a team member says that "orders are exploding," in the science of linguistics this is called a generalization (not specific). The generalization means something specific to the speaker, but is open to interpretation by everyone else. When people hear a generalization, they use their life experience to interpret the generalization into a specific fact. Their understanding is often quite different from what the speaker intended. Generalizations lead to team confusion.

What does "orders exploding" really mean? It could have a different meaning for each team member. Is it 100 orders or 10,000? Some team members might actually envision bombs going off in the shipping department. When you force the team to use the see, hear and feel filter you get a precise answer, like we have 400 orders shipping this month – a 35 percent increase over last year.

The see, hear and feel filter removes any ambiguity from the equation. When individuals disagree with the number, they can voice their concern or ask questions to get clarification. The discussion that results from this challenge helps the entire team get a better understanding of the actual situation.

If someone uses a generalization, any team member can ask for clarification. Here is a list of questions that you can use to get clarification:

- Can you say that in a different way?
- And that means?
- What specifically do you mean by that?
- How do you know this is accurate?

Questions give clarity to the entire team.

Remember, you can use questions like a hammer to hurt a teammate and show everyone how smart you are, or you can use questions like a flashlight to illuminate the truth for all.

As your team members start defining the current situation, write down the data on the whiteboard under the NOW circle. Remind your team it's their duty to the team to fully participate, offer input, and rigorously debate issues and ideas that end up of the whiteboard. There must be clarity and agreement on the facts before you move on to the next step in the process. The ideas and facts that are placed on the whiteboard will spark new insights and comments from the team that will further clarify the current situation (NOW).

As the leader, if you notice a team member who is not participating, reach out to that person and ask for input. Simple questions like:

- Janet, what do you think?
- Bob, how would you define it differently?
- Chloe, judging from your body language, do you see it differently?

When the whole team participates, there is greater clarity of the situation. This results in a more effective, and often more elegant solution. Finally, participation creates personal ownership of the solution so individual team members commit to the plan and execute it with passion.

Time to change roles

When the team runs out of ideas on ways to define the current situation, it's time to change roles from facilitator to mentor. If you start participating too early in the discussion, team members will stop thinking for themselves and will gladly use you as a crutch. "Why take a chance of looking stupid when the boss will do the thinking for me." Your status as the leader can also inhibit team members from challenging your ideas.

When you switch from a facilitator to a mentor, ask questions that illuminate gaps in the team's thinking so there is more clarity around the current (NOW) situation. This is your opportunity to bring up issues that the team has missed. Once your ideas are rigorously debated – perhaps challenged – they can be added to the whiteboard.

This serves two important functions for the team:

- They learn to think at a higher level
- They gain greater clarity of the current situation

Once the current situation is clearly defined, you must be sure that no relevant factors are missed. To accomplish this, read aloud the list of all the items that describe the current situation (NOW). Then ask the team: "What is missing from this list?" This simple question engages the "what's missing" filter, allowing team members to start looking for things that have been overlooked. You will be surprised at the amount of new information this simple question can bring to light.

When you think everyone agrees that the NOW situation is fully defined, get the team to sign off by asking: "We all agree this is the current situation, right?" Make sure you get a "yes" from everyone.

Note: If some team member say "yes," but you notice a little hesitation in their body language, call them on it. Everyone on the team must agree before you move on to the next step.

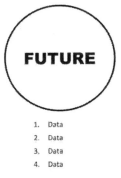

1. Data
2. Data
3. Data
4. Data

Step two: Defining the FUTURE

Now that you have defined the current situation (NOW), you are ready to move on to what the solution should look like (FUTURE).

On the upper right-hand side of the whiteboard, draw a circle and write the word FUTURE in it. This will prompt the team to define what the future (solution) looks like when the problem has been resolved.

Ask the team to describe what the solution (FUTURE) looks like if it were handled in the most ideal way. You can do this by asking questions like: "What does it look like if we solved it?", "What does it sound like?" and "What does it feel like?" As team members start describing the ideal state (FUTURE), write this information on the whiteboard under the Future circle. Invite them to challenge each other, especially when they need clarification of an idea. Let this process play out until the team runs out of ideas.

Take on the role of mentor again, and ask questions that illuminate gaps in the team's thinking so you help them find the ideal solution (FUTURE). Once again, take a more assertive role and bring up any ideas the team has overlooked. After your ideas are rigorously debated, add them to the whiteboard.

To ensure the solution state is fully defined, read through the entire list of what the FUTURE looks like. Then ask the team: "What's missing from this list?" If any new information comes out, have the team debate it and decide if it belongs on the whiteboard. Get everyone to sign off on the solution.

Think about what you have accomplished so far. In this simple, interactive process, everyone agrees on exactly what the problem is and what the solution looks like. This is the map that will guide the team to go from problem to solution, using the most effective route.

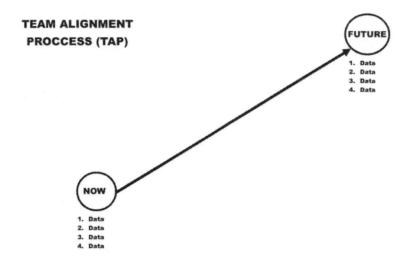

Step three: Draw the line

In psychological terms, the NOW circle on the whiteboard is a symbol that becomes a mental construct within the mind of each team member, one that clearly defines the problem. The FUTURE circle is a symbol that creates another mental construct, which clearly defines the solution within the mind on each team member. By connecting the two mental constructs, you make the solution seem easier to attain. And, you make this solution feel more real.

To connect the two constructs, start by saying to the team: "This is where we are now." Then take the team through the description of the current situation, which the team came up with. Tell the team, "This is where we are heading." Take the team through the description of the FUTURE that the team came up with. Finally, say to your team: "I guess this is the journey we are taking!" Then, with a touch of showmanship, draw a line from the NOW circle to the FUTURE circle.

This step is extremely important in the process because at a psychological level, what you are really doing is connecting the two mental constructs (problem to solution) in everyone's mind. At an unconscious level, you are also communicating the existence of a clear path to the solution. And, you're conveying a message that the solution is attainable by this team.

Step four: Limitations

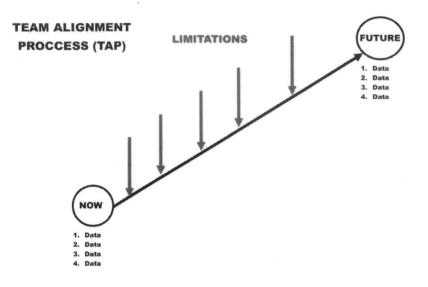

TEAM ALIGNMENT
PROCCESS (TAP)

LIMITATIONS

FUTURE

1. Data
2. Data
3. Data
4. Data

NOW

1. Data
2. Data
3. Data
4. Data

In this step, the team needs to clearly define limitations and challenges that could derail or get in the way of achieving success. Tell the team, "Alright! So what are the limitations or challenges that could get in the way of us making this happen?"

Team members will start listing potential obstacles to total success. It could be too little money, training or warehouse space. For each limitation, take a red marker and draw a red arrow pushing down on the line connecting the problem to the solution. Label each red line with its corresponding limitation. The longer the limitation line, the more serious that issue is.

Invite team members to challenge each other when someone mentions a limitation. This ensures that only true limitations end up on the whiteboard. Tell the team: "If you don't understand why this is a problem, ask for clarification." Often this type of discussion uncovers additional limitations that could sabotage the plan.

If any team member is silent during this part of the process, reach out to that person. "John, what else could get in the way? "Sally, is there something we are missing?"

After the team has exhausted all the limitations that need to be addressed, you are ready to help the team dig deeper. Ask the team the filter question: "Is there anything missing from this list?" Add any new items to the whiteboard that the team comes up with.

By switching to the mentor role, you can highlight any limitations that the team might have missed. Let the team discuss your suggestions as you maximize this teaching opportunity. Once again, ask the team if anything is missing. After all the limitations are listed, you end up with a set of red arrows pushing down on the path to the solution.

This visual representation can be quite sobering because it shows the magnitude of the problems that need to be overcome. Tell the team that each red arrow makes this journey tougher, and if not addressed properly, it could lead to failure.

Step five: Finding resources

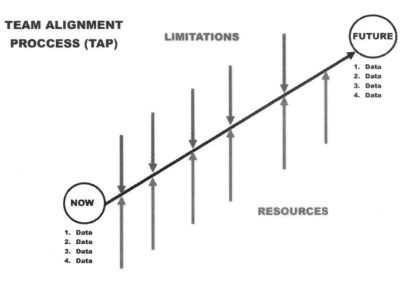

In this step, we clearly define the resources that the team needs to achieve success. To begin, tell the team: "We need to find the resources to overcome these limitations. The more resources we have, the faster we will achieve success."

Team members will start sharing the resources available or needed. The resources could range from talented people to strategic partnerships. They will start listing all the things they think could help. Use a green marker and draw a green arrow pushing up on the line that connects the problem to the solution. Label each green arrow with the resource name. The more important a resource is the longer line that represents it should be.

Invite team members to challenge one another so there is clarity and everyone is on the same page. Keep reminding team members to challenge each other at every stage of the process, which promotes a new habit. Debate ensures that only relevant information gets into the decision-making process. Just as important, all distracting irrelevant information never makes the cut. Let this process play out till the team has exhausted the list of available and needed resources.

Once again, if any of the team members are not participating in the conversation, reach out to them. "Dana, what else could help us achieve success?"

Use the "what's missing?" filter by listing aloud all the resources that are on the whiteboard. Then ask: "What's missing from this list?"

Once your team has exhausted a list of resources, switch to mentor mode. A good place to start is by pointing out red limitation lines that don't have a corresponding green resource to off-set them. Challenge the team to find creative ways to find needed resources. Once that is done, suggest other resources that could help the team to achieve success faster.

Finally, to ensure the team has not missed any crucial elements, ask the filter question again: "What is missing from this list?" What you'll end up with is a set of green arrows pushing up on the path that connects the NOW to the

FUTURE. The more green arrows you have, the faster you'll get to the solution.

A 360-Overview

In a few hours, you can guide your team to develop an overview that clearly defines a project. The overview includes:

- What the team views the problem to be
- What the team views the solution to be
- All limitations that could derail the project.
- All resources that lead to success.

Put the whiteboard data on a single sheet of paper and give it to all of the participants. Quite literally, this gets everyone on the same page.

Psychologically, having the problem and solution on a single sheet of paper leads people to think: "How tough could this be? Everything fits on just one piece of paper." This mindset can accelerate the team to success.

Step six: Building the action plan

"Success doesn't necessarily come from breakthrough innovation, but from flawless execution." Naveen Jain

Success always comes down to having a plan and executing it flawlessly. Up to this point, we have created a snapshot that encompasses the current situation (NOW), a desired outcome (FUTURE), limitations that need to be overcome and resources needed to succeed.

In this step of TAP, you will develop an action plan to guide your team to success.

Building an action plan

Ask the team: "What are the action steps required for success?" List the steps on a flip chart and organize them in the order in which they need to be executed. Then ask the team: "How do you know this is the first step?" If the team agrees that this particular action is the first step, then lock it in as step one. If the team uncovers a step previously missed, add it to the list in the appropriate location. To ensure that team members are on the same page, you must help them establish criteria that indicate success for each step of the plan.

To establish the criteria, ask the following question: "What do you need to see, hear or physically touch in order to know the task has been completed successfully?" As team members discuss the criteria, they will uncover any missing elements from the plan. It also brings clarity to the process so there are no missteps.

Then ask the team: "How do you know this is the next step?" If the team agrees, lock it in as the next step. If the team uncovers a missing element, make that the next step. Get the team to establish criteria for success for this step. This methodology ensures that your team develops a bullet-proof plan in which all team members are in lock-step.

Ask the team about any limitations they identified earlier that have not been addressed at this point. Get the team to insert action steps that address each limitation. Have the team establish the criteria so everyone knows what the successfully completed action looks like.

Use the same methodology to handle the steps to address any needed resources that have been missed. Once the team is satisfied with the plan, add any missing elements and criteria that you think will make the plan better. It's another opportunity to teach the team to think at a higher level.

Finally, read the steps and the associated criteria out loud for each step of the plan and ask: "Is there anything missing from this plan?" If there is a missing element, add that to the plan. You are now ready to share the plan with rest of your organization.

If the plan is complex with a lot of moving parts, you can plug this data into a project management tool like Microsoft Project or Virtual Project Office. Otherwise, you can use something as simple as a Google Docs spreadsheet. Make sure every team member brings the 360-overview to each meeting because this is the glue that keeps the team on the same page and going in the same direction.

Step Seven: The Past

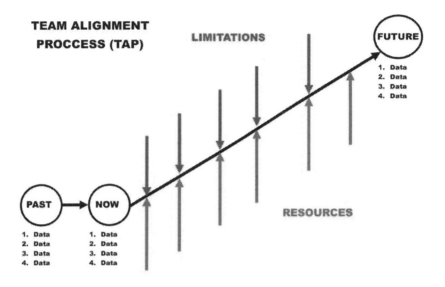

"Those who cannot remember the past are condemned to repeat it". George Santayana

There is one other element that can add value to the Team Alignment Process. The past gives us insight as to how we arrived at the NOW space.

In this step we learn from the past in order to accelerate our journey to the FUTURE. Here are some questions that will help you learn from the past:

- What worked well and where did we struggle?
- What was the situation back then?
- What assumptions did we make?
- How did we make those assumptions?

- Were they correct?
- Did we see ourselves reaching the FUTURE spot by now?
- If not, what got in the way?

Go to the white board and draw a circle to the left of the NOW circle. Tell the team that this circle represents the past. Start the conversation with: "Okay! Six months ago when we started this project, what was the situation like? What did it look like then? What did it sound like? What did it feel like? What were the assumptions we made?" In this part of the process, you want the team in agreement as to how to define the situation in the PAST and how we got to the current state (NOW).

I know I am being repetitive in the following section, but it is essential to the process to follow the same steps each time you lead the team.

Tell your team members that it's their duty to the team to fully participate, offer input, and rigorously debate issues and ideas that end up on the whiteboard. There must be clarity and agreement as to the exact nature of the past situation. Participants must ask for clarifications when they need it. As the process plays out, new insights that are placed on the whiteboard will spark the team to gain further clarity.

As team members start defining the past situation, write down this information on the whiteboard.

Get everyone to participate. Once everybody has participated and has a solid understanding of the past situation, then and only then, add any missing elements. Get everyone to sign off on the PAST, indicating that we all agree this is where we were X months ago.

Team Alignment Process: Overview

STEP 1 (Use black pen): Draw the NOW circle on the lower left hand side of the whiteboard or sheet of paper. Ask your team members to define the NOW space. What is the problem? Define it! What does it look like? What does it sound like? What does it feel like? Record the ideas below the NOW circle.

Let the team members know that it's not only okay to ask for clarification, it's their duty to the team to make sure everyone understands. Tell them its okay to challenge each other because having a rigorous debate is the best way to ensure no stone is left unturned. Once your team has clearly defined what's going on NOW and all discussion has stopped, you can ask the filter question.

Read the list out loud and ask: "What's missing from this list?" The team will add any missing items. Then and only then, you can add any items that the team has missed up to this point. Your ideas must be discussed and agreed upon before they are recorded on the whiteboard or paper. Once the NOW space has been fully defined and everyone has signed off on it, you can go to step two.

STEP 2 (Use black pen): Go to the upper right hand side of the whiteboard or paper. Draw the FUTURE circle there. Ask the team members to define what the solution looks like. What does it sound like? What does it feel like? Encourage rigorous debate and record all the data that is generated. Add any items that your team has missed, encourage more debate and record the data. Then ask: "What's missing from this list?

Most of the time, the group will generate additional ideas. Let the group debate the additions and record the result under the FUTURE space. Once the FUTURE space has been fully defined and everyone has signed off on it, you can go to step three.

STEP 3 (Use black pen): Don't underestimate the power of this simple step. Draw a line from the NOW space to the FUTURE space. This accomplishes the following:

- This solution is more possible because you have connected the problem and the solution in the minds of team members. It's a done deal!

- The straight line infers that it's not going to be difficult. People think: "If we think clearly and we follow this right path, we can't go wrong." Now we can move on to step 4.

STEP 4 (Use red pen): Step four is where we define limitations that could sabotage success. Ask the team: "What are the things that are going to get in the way of us reaching the FUTURE (solution state)? What are the things that we don't have that we need to have in order to be successful?"

Ask your team to list those limitations; once again it is okay to ask for clarification, to challenge each other, to talk out these issues. Record each limitation with an arrow and label it using a red pen. Once all the limitations are recorded, add any items that your team has missed. Using red represent limitations kicks in the reptile brain of your teammates so they are driven to make the red go away because it is "dangerous".

Then ask your team: "Is there anything important missing from this list, something that we need to know?" Discuss any additions and get everyone to sign off on it before you go to step five.

STEP 5 (Use green pen): Ask the team to list the resources you have or need in order to off-set the limitation and successfully complete the project. Resources could include strategic partnerships that you have in the industry, consultants, internal resources and money. Once team members have finished a list of resources, add any elements they have missed. Once again, it is okay to ask for clarification and have a rigorous debate about the issues.

Once everything has been listed, read through the resources and ask the question: "What is missing from this list?" Add in any items that the team missed and get the team to sign off on the resources.

At this point, we have the whole situation clearly defined and everyone on the team is on the same page, going in the same direction. Now it's time to turn this 360-overview into an action plan.

Creating action steps

To begin building the action plan, recap the work done so far:

- The NOW
- The FUTURE
- The LIMITATIONS
- The RESOURCES

Ask the team, "What are the steps that we need to take to solve this problem?" Once the team has finished, add any elements they have missed. Once again, it is okay to ask for clarifications and have a rigorous debate about the issues.

Then ask the team: "What LIMITATIONS do we need to eliminate or reduce? The more limitations we offset or remove the faster we arrive at the solution."

Follow with another question for the team: "What RESOURCES do we need to add or enhance. The more RESOURCES we have the faster we arrive at the solution."

Some of the action steps that come out of this process will be simple and straightforward, while others will require more time and manpower. For example, a new intake process would need input from five departments including IT. It might take two weeks to get all the right people in a room to work on the problem. It might take two additional months to lock down a procedure that everyone agrees upon. The IT component could be a process by itself.

My point here is that the 360-overview keeps everyone from getting lost in the weeds. The action steps can be plugged into project-management software to ensure all the details are addressed and the project is on time and on budget. As the steps are completed, they are checked off on the 360-overview.

NOTE: Two case histories that illustrate the elegance of TAP are available online at

http://nolimitsselling.com/crazysexy

CONCLUSION

Everything in this world is speeding up. For example, it took radio 75 years to reach 50 million users (radio sets). Angry Birds hit the 50 million user mark in 35 days. In a 2010 interview, Eric Schmidt, the CEO of Google said, "Every two days now we create as much information as we did from the dawn of civilization up until 2003."

In this brave new world we have 3D printers that can print human organs. We have a better understanding of the cosmos. Every field of study is making advances at a staggering rate. All these new ideas, products and services need to be sold.

Face-to-face selling has been unchanged in any meaningful way for decades. The reason for this stagnation is that the sales process works pretty well. The issue isn't sales training. The issue is getting salespeople to follow directions in the manner prescribed by sales gurus.

The old adage that you can lead a horse to water but you can't make her drink, sums up the problem. Salespeople are driven and they want to excel in their profession. They want more money, more recognition, to make a difference in the world. To get better results they pay good money to be shown how to get to the "water" (sales training), but fear and hesitation stop them from drinking it.

To significantly advance sales performance we need to empower salespeople with tools that will allow them to breakthrough their barriers. They need a stronger mindset so they can wholeheartedly execute their sales training and sales strategies.

The latest advances in neuroscience give us the understanding and the toolkit to help salespeople breakthrough their self-imposed barriers and get the mindset they need to be successful.

I wrote this book to give you the foundation to explore this new frontier. I have shared the best models to describe human behavior including the three main areas were salespeople get stuck. In chapter 12, I have shared a NeuroBooster that will help you to access peak states of performance so you can get more done. In chapter 13, I share a NeuroBooster that will help you get unstuck. This is ideally suited for small issues that get in the way of your performance.

FREE Advanced Mind Training

For readers who want to do a deeper dive into this subject, I have created an advanced online learning portal. There you will learn how to break through any mental barrier that gets in the way of your sales performance. Here are some of the advanced skills that you will learn:

- How to let go of past mistakes
- How to boost your self-esteem
- Improve your critical thinking
- And more

Get Your Free Mind Training Here:

http://tinyurl.com/za8s8sh

ABOUT THE AUTHOR

My purpose in life is to help people breakthrough their barriers so they build happier, more successful lives.

A mentor once asked me, "What's the wow in your work?' The wow for me is when a client tells me I changed their life for the better. This is what fuels me. This is the reason I do what I do.

I love learning new things and sharing my new-found wisdom with the world. I live for making connections between ideas that give me a deeper understanding of the subject matter.

I'm a great motivational speaker and have had the privilege of presenting my ideas to audiences in 14 countries.

I have over 24 years of experience being a business and sales consultant. Since 2003, I have been using NLP to change human behavior for individuals and teams.

I am one part business guru, one part change expert who has a strong intuitive sense of uncovering the right solution.

The most important thing you need to know about me is that I am happiest when I am helping people break through their barriers.

Recommended Resources

An invitation-only organization for Baltimore's best sales leaders.

We bring together Baltimore's highest performing sales leaders into an exclusive group of peers that support each other by sharing insights, best practices and real world solutions to commonly held challenges.

- Join a trusted, vetted peer forum where you can leverage the wisdom of equally successful executives
- Access member driven research and best practice solutions to commonly held challenges
- Find solutions to problems faster and cheaper than via consultants
- Learn from member experiences and avoid making the same costly mistakes
- Participate in thought leadership events and speaker series

410-949-7067

www.TheLeaderBoard.com

We are a creative team of problem solvers dedicated to providing exceptional construction services to our clients. Rocchi becomes your virtual construction department. We use the Design-Build methodology of construction. Design-Build gives you one point of contact that oversees your entire project from initial concept through completion.

Design-Build Delivers:
- Get initial design upfront so you know what the end project will look like
- Get an accurate budget before the project starts
- Get an accurate schedule before the project starts
- No finger pointing between architects and contractors when problems occur
- Less Hassel - projects completed on time and on budget

(410) 252-9430

www.RocchiUSA.com

Solutions Customized for Your Business

We are a full-service IT/Security/Communications company focused on delivering technology services and solutions to businesses across the USA. We offer specialized, highly customized technological solutions for small and medium sized businesses. Our experienced team will be able to assist you in creating a practical, sustainable infrastructure for your business, from helping develop your overall IT Strategy down to implementing a fully functional Surveillance System in your environment.

We are your go-to solution for:
- IT services
- Cybersecurity
- Security and access solutions protecting your environment
- Secure, IP based telephony systems for your business

(410) 559-7020

www.sostechgroup.com

CATAPULT YOUR THINKING, BUSINESS, AND LIFE.

We offer shared office space for creatives.

Hang out with the creative class. Writers, artists, photographers, fashion designers, innovators, small business owners... Inspire and get inspired by collaborating with really smart people.

Participate in roundtables with industry gurus that will help you accelerate the growth of your company. Get introduced to thought leaders, entrepreneurs and investors at our networking events. Use our studio to create podcasts, webinars and videos to share your expertise with the world. Come join us, grab an open desk and get to work. There is coffee, tea and a boatload of expertize and motivation to keep you fueled.

- Guidance from industry gurus
- Strong community
- Business & social events
- Pathway to investors

(443) 470-9029

www.catapultspace